RESILIENT
MIND

ACHIEVE SUCCESS BY BUILDING MENTAL
AND EMOTIONAL TOUGHNESS

BRAD COULBECK

HIBBERT & STILES
PUBLISHING INC.

Hibbert & Stiles Publishing Inc.
PO Box 35016 Nelson Park R. O.
London, Ontario N5W 5Z6
www.hspubinc.com

Ordering information for print editions:
Quantity sales. Special discounts may be available on quantity purchases by corporations, associations, and others. For details, contact publisher.

Cover and interior design by D.E. West - ZAQ Designs

2017 Hibbert & Stiles Publishing Edition
The Resilient Mind: Achieve Success by Building Mental and Emotional Toughness / Brad Coulbeck

Publisher's Cataloging-In-Publication Data
(Prepared by The Donohue Group, Inc.)

Names: Coulbeck, Brad.
Title: The resilient mind : achieve success by building mental and emotional toughness / Brad Coulbeck.
Description: 2017 Hibbert & Stiles Publishing edition. | London, Ontario : Hibbert & Stiles Publishing Inc., [2017]
Identifiers: ISBN 978-1-988353-55-5 (print) | ISBN 978-1-988353-56-2 (ebook)
Subjects: LCSH: Resilience (Personality trait) | Toughness (Personality trait) | Mental discipline. | Stress management. | Success.
Classification: LCC BF698.35.R47 C68 2017 (print) | LCC BF698.35.R47 (ebook) | DDC 155.24--dc23

www.hspubinc.com

THE
RESILIENT
MIND

DEDICATION

This book is dedicated to my two mentally tough and independent children, Melissa and Ryan.

CONTENTS

INTRODUCTION

"I take the Kassam rocket, the instrument of death, and I
change it… I transfer it into something of beauty."
Yaron Bob, sculptor and artist

If you ever feel stressed because of the many competing demands of the modern workplace…if you ever feel overwhelmed with the pressures of family, work, and finances…and
if you ever worry or have anxiety about the future, *then you're not
alone*. According to researchers at Carnegie Mellon University,
37 percent of US adults feel overwhelmed by stress. Seventeen
percent of men and 24 percent of women report *extreme* stress.

We are living in the most demanding time in human history. There were certainly other periods of history when quality
of life was much worse; however, there has never been a time
when people had so many demands and such unrelenting pressure. Consider the rate at which information is coming at you:
It's like drinking from a fire hose. There is more public scrutiny

and accountability than ever before. If you messed up twenty years ago, you could hide it; now everyone has a video camera on their smart phone. When good people do bad things, they can immediately become an overnight sensation when it goes viral on social media—all just because of a momentary slip in judgment. Being "switched on" 24/7 is the new reality; your boss can always reach you on your Blackberry or Android. Doing more with less has become cliché.

The cost to us is *stress*.

I have experienced my share of stress in my twenty-five years as a police officer. But the source of most of the stress isn't what people expect. In a study done by Linda Duxbury of Carleton University and Christopher Higgins of Western University, they found that of the forty-five hundred officers from twenty-five police agencies studied:

- A typical officer works 53.5 hours per week.

- 46 percent agreed that the culture within their workforce emphasizes work over family.

- 50 percent report high stress levels, while 46 percent report moderate stress levels.[1]

They also found that the majority of a cop's stress is *organizational*, not *operational*. A police officer's job is extremely complex, requiring a wide breadth of knowledge to handle the rapid and dramatic changes that happen every day. The very po-

---

1) Quan, D. (2012, January 1). Canadian police officers overworked, understaffed, stressed-out: Survey. Retrieved from www.canada.com.

lice station itself can be a hotbed for workplace conflict, human resource issues, and toxic people. So, the majority of a police officer's stress is not unlike the stress faced by anyone working in the modern workplace.

On an average workday, at least half of all employees feel some kind of work-related stress. Fifty percent of all sick time is linked to stress, either directly or indirectly. (Indirectly because when you are stressed, your immune system is compromised. You may get the flu because of stress and not even know the cause.)

What is the answer to all this chronic and cumulative stress? The answer is not simply slowing down and smelling the roses—not if you want to achieve your goals. The answer is learning how to *reduce* stress *without* reducing your demands.

Because, after all, it's the high demands that make you successful.

The only solution for goal-oriented people is to build the capacity to deal with the pressure and stress of today's world without suffering the adverse effects of stress. This is achievable by increasing "resiliency."

You will face obstacles and adversity in your career. I guarantee it. You can only reach your success potential by having the grit to keep going during times of immense stress, and by having the resiliency to take a hit and keep moving forward.

But typical, everyday stress is not the only problem. In addition to our own demanding lives, there are dangers around us, and because of modern media, we have access to all the gory details. Terrorists, extremists, and militants gather in dark corners, envisioning grand plans of medieval conquest. ISIS is crossing the Middle East, leaving a trail of carnage. Totalitarian governments that are sworn enemies of the West are working toward nuclear weapon capabilities. Closer to home there are lone-wolf terrorist attacks and violent, video-game-playing loners going on killing sprees before they kill themselves.

Many survivors of wars and violence face the aftermath every day. Even though the bombs and bullets have stopped flying, their inner battle continues. Silent struggle wears them down, making normalcy appear to be unreachable. Even amid external peace, they find themselves tied to the memories of devastating destruction. For some, experiencing *distress* is an everyday happening.

If any country understands conflict it is the State of Israel, which has been at war regularly since 1947. In this war-torn land, the blood of many people cries for ceasefire. They are only vaguely familiar with the concept of peace.

Yet beauty can emerge from conflict; you just have to look for it. Yaron Bob, an artist and sculptor, takes Kassam rockets and turns them into beautiful roses whose petals speak of a hope for a better tomorrow.

Post-Traumatic Stress Disorder (PTSD) is not a given when you experience trauma. After trauma a higher percentage of people experience Post-Traumatic Growth (PTG) than experience PTSD. (A majority of people have never heard of PTG, but a later chapter will examine this more closely.) Most people are naturally resilient, and will bounce back after trauma. We can increase our resilience even more through education and training.

It's safe to say that everyone will experience stress at some time in their life. This book will use scientific research and practical experience to help you combat that stress and increase the resiliency you need to handle it effectively. It will teach you how to succeed in the fast-paced, no-holds-barred environment we live in, thereby improving your happiness in life. My aim is to teach you:

- How to thrive in a psychologically demanding environment

- How to bounce back quickly after personal or professional disaster

- How to increase your mental and emotional strength

- How to improve your health by reducing harmful stress hormones

- How to adapt to traumatic and chronic stress

- How you can achieve peak performance while under stress, and

- How to overcome obstacles and flourish in your professional and personal life.

After reading this book, you will be more mentally and emotionally tough, and better able to face life's challenges with the assurance that you have the power to succeed in today's world.

NOTE ON THE MIDDLE EAST CONFLICT

In the book I use examples of Israeli resiliency programs in areas where civilians have been subject to Kassam rocket attacks. This was not meant to villainize those from the Palestinian Territories, or to take sides in the conflict. There are victims and injustices on both sides, and loving people and good friends of mine in both Israel and the West Bank. I used the Israeli examples simply because of the available research, the positive outcomes they achieved, and to illustrate specific points I was making.

PART ONE
RESILIENCY

CHAPTER ONE

WHAT IS RESILIENCY?

"The greatest weapon against stress is our ability to
choose one thought over another."
William James (1842–1910), author and psychologist

Stress is the leading cause of illness in North America. According to the American Psychological Association (APA), chronic stress is linked to the six leading causes of death: heart disease, cancer, lung ailments, accidents, cirrhosis of the liver, and suicide. Stress can have a significant negative impact on our lives—professionally and personally—if we don't have strategies to cope.

Much of the stress management literature out there is about lowering our demands. That is *not* what I teach. I believe that the high demands that we place on ourselves are the aspects of life that make us successful. We need these stresses and challenges if we want to live fully!

STRESS DEFINED

Let's talk about what stress is and how it affects your health. WebMD has this to say about stress:

> *The human body is designed to experience stress and react to it. Stress can be positive, keeping us alert and ready to avoid danger. Stress becomes negative when a person faces continuous challenges without relief or relaxation between challenges. As a result, the person becomes overworked and stress-related tension builds.*[1]

In the case of a short-term incident or in an emergency, such as in battle or on the scene of an accident, stress hormones (adrenaline and cortisol) help us. They boost immunity and make us stronger so that we can survive the adverse situation. They also give us energy and keep us focused. But over the long term, if we chronically have too much adrenaline and cortisol in our system, it is bad for us on many different levels, emotionally, physically, and cognitively. Dr. Linda Duxbury of Carleton University says that the stressful day-to-day grind is more damaging stress than traumatic stress, based on her research of thousands of police officers. Our bodies were designed to handle stress on a short-term basis, not for the long term[2].

Excess stress, or "distress," as it is often called, can lead to the following behavioral and physical effects:

---

1) The Effects of Stress on Your Body. (2014, June 24). Retrieved from www.webmd.com.
2) L. Duxbury, C. Higgins (2012, March) Caring for and about those who serve: Work-life conflict and employee well-being within Canada's Police Departments.

Behavioral Effects

- Depression
- Foggy thinking
- Anxiety
- Lowered performance
- Procrastination
- Lack of motivation
- Lack of concentration
- Impaired memory
- Lack of focus
- Feeling overwhelmed
- Insomnia
- Aggression

Physical Effects

- Compromised immune system
- Excess cortisol and adrenaline in system, causing other problems, such as neurons in the brain not binding
- Prolonged exposure to cortisol, which devastates the immune system
- Prolonged elevation of stress hormones, which can result in insulin resistance and diabetes
- Belly fat

- Increased heart attack risk

- Stomach problems

- Fatigue

- Tension

So, how does resiliency play a part in de-stressing your life?

RESILIENCY DEFINED

Let's take a look at what resiliency is to get a better picture of the key to its potent bounce-back power. The American Psychological Association defines being resilient as:

> ...the process of adapting well in the face of adversity, trauma, tragedy, threats or significant sources of stress—such as family and relationship problems, serious health problems or workplace and financial stressors. It means "bouncing back" from difficult experiences.[3]

We all suffer failure from time to time, whether in business, relationships, health, etc. I've had my share, starting with eleventh grade math! However, our success in life isn't determined by whether we fail or not; it's determined by how we react to that failure. After we suffer the typical tailspin and a period of distress or malaise, do we bounce back? Or do we sink deeper into hopelessness?

---

3) The Road to Resilience. (n.d.). Retrieved January 13, 2015, from www.apa.org.

Resilient people bounce back. Remember, challenges are short term, but success is long term.

A fundamental question, then, is "Can resiliency be taught?" The answer is "Yes," according to Dr. Martin Seligman, professor at the University of Pennsylvania, and author of several books on the topic of positive psychology. He is involved in a program with the US military that is teaching resiliency and mental toughness to sergeants and other boots-on-the-ground leaders. The goal is to decrease PTSD and increase well-being and Post-Traumatic Growth. The skills they are teaching also work well for leaders in other fields.

RESILIENCE VS. STRESS RESISTANCE

Resilience is the ability to adapt to significant adversity and trauma, to recover quickly, to bounce back. Resilient individuals may indeed have a stress reaction after going through a traumatic incident. They may go into a tailspin and suffer temporary symptoms such as sleeplessness, shock, anxiety, disbelief, and depression—but it is temporary, and within a short period of time, usually, they get back to normal. It may not be the same state as before, rather an adapted state that is a little higher or lower than the old emotional state, a "new normal." But it is a state of homeostasis, and the individual will be fully functioning.

A non-resilient individual, by contrast, would not recover from the tailspin and would not get back to a normal of any kind. They would most likely have long-term functional impairments and, potentially, PTSD.

Now, a person who has a high level of stress *resistance* would never have the tailspin in the first place. Whatever the crisis is, it would just be a small blip on the screen of their lives and then life as normal continues without any acute stress reaction.

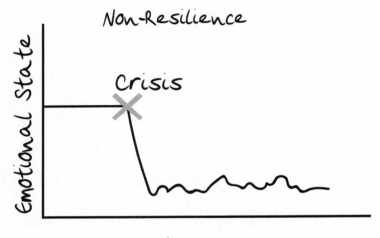

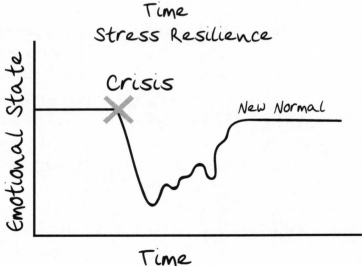

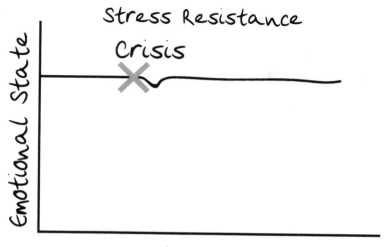

These charts illustrate the difference between being non-resilient, resilient, and stress resistant.

Isn't it better to be resistant to stress instead of resilient, then?

Not in all circumstances. After going through serious trauma, it would be normal and natural to have some stress reaction. That's what makes us human. If you don't have some acute stress reaction after a loved one dies, then you might be a psychopath! Although I like much of the Stoic philosophy, I don't recommend just shutting off our negative emotions. The full human experience involves stress and grieving and it is good to feel a full range of emotions.

The place we do need to develop stress resistance is in our regular work and family life. People that suffer stress reactions from routine day-to-day issues will potentially develop psychological and physiological problems needlessly. It's perfectly legitimate to allow yourself to react to the stress you experience when you go through a significant trauma in life, but it's not good when your reaction is from dealing with a bad boss that you see every day.

The healthiest and most ideal mindset, then, is to be resilient in some circumstances and stress resistant in others.

Resistance and resilience are developed in the same way. Incorporating resiliency factors into your life will grow your levels of both resistance and resilience. Resiliency factors are behavioral characteristics that can be learned that make a person impervious to the negative effects of stress.

Throughout the rest of this book, I will discuss the various characteristics and behaviors that will make you immune to the stress caused by the demands of the modern workplace. These characteristics and behaviors will also give you the ability to bounce back after a major crushing blow in your life. For the purpose of clarity, from here on I will refer to stress resistance and resiliency simply as "resiliency," since there is no need to differentiate the two. Their positive outcomes are the same.

Let me leave this opening chapter with a personal experience, demonstrating these concepts.

On the 4th of July 2011, I spent the day in Sderot, a beautiful Israeli town of about twenty-five thousand people on the border of the Gaza Strip, only three miles from Gaza City. Because of its unfortunate geographic location, it has been a target of Hamas and other terrorist groups in Gaza; since 2001, over eleven thousand Kassam rockets have been fired at Sderot, with over fourteen hundred of them landing in the town.

The people of Sderot live under constant threat. During my time there, it seemed like such a normal, peaceful town. I might have forgotten the threat level if it wasn't for the reminders everywhere: every bus shelter was a concrete bunker, and there were bunkers beside all the playgrounds and other public buildings. When the "Red Color" alarm sounds, people only have fifteen seconds to get inside a bunker, which explains why they are needed everywhere.

A common question from Westerners to the inhabitants is, "Why don't you move?" It's not that easy. They were born and raised there; their lives, their jobs, their businesses, and homes are there. But more than that, many of the residents will express a shared sentiment: "We don't let the Kassams control us." I like that. That is an attitude of resilience, an attitude of feeling in control, as opposed to feeling like a helpless victim.

There are other aspects of resilience that we can learn from Sderot. All the elementary school children have witnessed the rocket attacks, leaving 44 percent of the children with PTSD at the time of one study a few years ago. The Israel Center for the Treatment of Psychotrauma started "Parent's Place," a safe place for mothers and children to go and take part in programs that build resilience. Often, parents don't play with children when they are under threat; it seems like a luxury they don't have. But at Parent's Place the mothers and children take part in programs involving music, drama, crafts, and art, which help them relax and release stress, and find meaning. They also play together, which builds the relationship between the children and their mothers, providing a strengthened support system that is a major protective factor against traumatic stress. The result has been a reduced rate of PTSD in these children.

One of the major stresses for the children is the "Red Color" alarm. Even when the rockets miss the town, the alarm itself causes psychological injury. Children cry, scream, sometimes freeze, which is very dangerous when they have only fifteen seconds to get to safety. One of the ingenious ideas at one school was the creation of a song for the children to sing as they react to the alarm. It's an active song with actions that helps them to focus on what they need to do and validates their physiological and psychological reactions to the stress. It helps them feel the support of their friends, and ends with "shaking it out," breathing exercises, laughing, and celebrating that the rocket missed them and they are safe. It sounds awful that kindergarten children should have to sing a song like that... but it's ingenious in the way it incorporates so many resiliency factors into a song. Ultimately, it has had a positive outcome because it has reduced the stress and anxiety of the school kids during and after the alarms.

The day before I was in Sderot, a rocket was fired from Gaza into the Sderot region. The day after I was there, two militants were killed in Gaza by an Israeli airstrike as they prepared to launch a rocket. The attacks still continue.

If the mothers and children of Sderot can be so resilient in the face of such constant threat, then how can we not learn to overcome the smaller stresses we have in our daily lives?

CHAPTER TWO
WHY DOES RESILIENCY MATTER?

"Resiliency, not perfection, is the signature of greatness,
be it in a person, an organization, or a nation."
Jim Collins, Built to Last

For centuries, man has wrestled with how to recuperate from the devastating events that sometimes happen in life. Your ability to bounce back after these traumatic events dictates your capacity to build a productive, successful life; therefore, being resilient is a critical ingredient in success. Diane Coutu, author of a Harvard Business Review article quoting Dean Becker, says:

> *More than education, more than experience, more than training, a person's level of resilience will determine who succeeds and who fails. It's true in the cancer ward, it's true in the Olympics, and it's true in the boardroom.*[4]

---

4) Coutu, D. (2002, May 1). How Resilience Works. Retrieved from hbr.org.

Building resiliency is sometimes like flexing a muscle that doesn't see much action. It requires quite a bit of work, but the benefits outweigh the sacrifice. Personal growth does not come from doing that which is easy. There is no growth without adversity. Rocky, in the movie *Rocky Balboa,* had it right when he gave this advice to his son:

> *The world ain't all sunshine and rainbows. It's a very mean and nasty place, and I don't care how tough you are, it will beat you to your knees and keep you there permanently if you let it. You, me, or nobody is gonna hit as hard as life. But it ain't about how hard you hit. It's about how hard you can get hit and keep moving forward. How much you can take and keep moving forward. That's how winning is done.*

If you want to succeed in the game of life, you must master the art of being resilient. Wanting an easy life is not practical or probable in the twenty-first century. Instead of procrastinating or running from your priorities when demands become overwhelming, it is possible to increase your capacity to finish them successfully. You lower stress by increasing your resilience and building that muscle so that when life happens, you are ready for it.

In the book *The Obstacle is the Way,* author Ryan Holiday says:

We've all done it. Said: "I am so [overwhelm-ed, tired, stressed, busy, blocked, outmatched]." And then what do we do about it? Go out and party. Or treat ourselves. Or sleep in. Or wait. It feels better to ignore or pretend. But you know deep down that that isn't going to truly make it any better. You've got to act. And you've got to start now.

Successful people have stress in their lives *because* they place high demands on themselves. In order to continue on their path to achievement, they have to enhance their ability to deal with a high demand, as opposed to reducing their demands in order to quell the stress.

Successful people possess the following characteristics:

- Drive
- Self-reliance
- Willpower
- Passion
- Competitive spirit
- Grit
- Optimism
- Courage
- Determination
- Self-confidence

These characteristics require making a demand of yourself. But it's only by pushing yourself and facing pain and stepping outside your comfort zone that will allow you to reach your true potential.

There are times when you can reduce your demands, but you have to be strategic about it. Reduce the demands that don't serve to move you ahead, that don't do anything for you. But keep the high demands that will lift you to your success potential.

THE COST OF WORKPLACE STRESS

Today's business environment is psychologically demanding. To be successful you have to be able to thrive in this environment. Contrary to popular belief, law enforcement—my background—is not very different from most corporations when it comes to sources of stress. Many people outside of law enforcement attribute its job-related stress to the trauma, gruesome scenes, dangerous situations, and high risk of death. True, there is stress in those situations, but as I mentioned in the introduction, research has shown that about 80 percent of the stress in policing is *organizational* as opposed to *operational*. It's the human resources issues—relations with coworkers, toxic employees, tyrannical bosses. These stressors are, of course, very similar to the stress that most employees face in a corporate environment.

There is also the cycle of family stress that affects the workplace, and the other way around. For example, when you are going through a difficult time in an intimate relationship, it makes it hard to focus at work. Your work performance may suffer, which can cause stress at work, which you also take back home. This then increases the stress at home, which multiplies the stress everywhere else in a vicious cycle. It's the same if you are going through a very difficult time at work, and you bring that stress home to your family. It has a negative impact on your family life, which then just makes it worse going back to work because you don't feel support on the home front.

Fiscal and emotional costs due to stress from absenteeism, medical expenses, and lost productivity are steadily growing in almost every industry in North America. Some recent research states the following:

- "Forty-three percent of all adults suffer adverse health effects from stress.

- Seventy-five percent to 90 percent of all doctor's office visits are for stress-related ailments and complaints.

- Stress can play a part in problems such as headaches, high blood pressure, heart problems, diabetes, skin conditions, asthma, arthritis, depression, and anxiety.

- The Occupational Safety and Health Administration (OSHA) declared stress a hazard of the workplace. Stress costs American industry more than $300 billion annually.

- The lifetime prevalence of an emotional disorder is more than 50 percent, often due to chronic, untreated stress reactions."[5]

My personal beliefs about resiliency are derived from various books and research articles I've studied, courses I've taken, and experiences that I've had. I've learned that resilient people have the grit to thrive despite adversity. They flourish in a psychologically demanding work environment because of their mental and emotional toughness.

The world is a stressful place. In the past, I have seen adversity not only in my own life but in the lives of my family, friends, and coworkers. Witnessing trauma, work stress, adversity, and financial crises in my life and in the lives of others encouraged me to seek a resolution. I realized that you have to be able to handle adversity because it is an integral fiber of everyone's life.

In order to come out on the winning side of adversity, you must possess or acquire resiliency factors, which are defined in the upcoming chapters. It is my observation that some people come wired with many of these traits and others, with some diligence, can acquire them in order to become more resilient.

For example, more people are beginning to realize now that leadership can be taught. While there are those that are born with leadership qualities, it can also be learned by others. It's the same with resiliency: many are born with resilient qualities, but it can also be learned. I was surprised once I started learning about it myself. It had never hit me before that you could adjust your personality and behavior to become impervious to certain kinds of stress.

I've faced stress on all levels, professionally and personally.

5) The Effects of Stress on Your Body. (2014, June 24). Retrieved from www.webmd.com.

Sixteen years ago, when I was first promoted to a supervisory position and had to deal with toxic people in the workplace, it caused me to experience insomnia and anger. I realize now that they didn't cause my anger. It was my interpretation and beliefs that caused my reaction. I still deal with the same problems today in my current work, but it doesn't cause the same reaction anymore, and I no longer lose sleep because of work issues.

There are certain factors that have been an innate part of my personality my entire life. For instance, I've always been an optimistic person. I've always believed in God, or a higher power. I've always been able to step back and look at the eternal perspective. I've had a good support system within my immediate family. I've had these resiliency factors in my life all along, but I did not realize it because they were inherent.

My journey toward understanding resiliency, and realizing that I could do more to be proactive and build my own resiliency, began around 2006. I took a course from Dr. Bill McDermott, a psychologist, who touched on resiliency at one point, even though the class was not focused on that topic. I talked to him about it afterward, and from there I started studying the concept in great depth. Over the last ten years I've been building my own resiliency.

It's not just about an academic endeavor for me. It has resulted in a positive life change that has driven me toward success. And by success I not only mean professional success, but also increased happiness and peace in life. When you start this journey, it can do the same for you.

Why does resiliency matter? It matters because your success and your happiness matter!

CHAPTER THREE
HOW DO YOU BECOME RESILIENT?

"The world breaks everyone, and afterward,
some are strong at the broken places."
Ernest Hemingway, A Farewell to Arms

It has been established in the previous chapters that resiliency is one of the key factors in living a successful life, regardless of your occupation.

As I mentioned before, most people are naturally resilient, but for those who are not, resiliency can be learned and increased over a period of time. People who do not possess the innate capacity for resiliency can acquire it through training.

Before we continue, though, it might be helpful to debunk another myth. I have read articles where the authors have said that PTSD is the normal reaction to trauma. That is simply not true. Often those who say that are people who have suffered with PTSD themselves...but quite honestly, the science just doesn't support that view.

THE TRUTH ABOUT PTSD

In 2011, George Bonnano, a leading resilience researcher from Columbia University, wrote that the single most common outcome after a traumatic event is "recovery without intervention." Research shows that *most* people recover after trauma without any kind of treatment. In other words, most people are naturally resilient.

It is normal to have some type of stress reaction after trauma, but in the vast majority of cases, those reactions are temporary. Most people will experience some type of physiological or emotional reaction after severe stress, at the very least due to the adrenaline dump into their system. They may have feelings of shock, horror, or disbelief and may experience hyperarousal, emotional numbing, or trouble sleeping. These various reactions are reasonable to expect and usually subside within a few weeks, *without* turning into full-on PTSD. Most research shows that PTSD rates after a traumatic event are in the neighborhood of 8 to 20 percent (torture and rape excluded, which have higher rates). That means that 80 to 90 percent of people do not develop PTSD after experiencing trauma[6].

That is good news.

The other positive news is that PTSD is actually preventable in many cases. Prevention can be accomplished through resiliency training pre-incident, and also through post-incident support. In one study (Brewin et al, 2000), researchers found that the severity of the trauma had less to do with the outcome than the support the victim received after the event. A lack of support after trauma, as we will see in the next chapter, is a

6) S. Benish, Z. Imel, B Wampold (2007) N. Roberts, N. Kitchiner. J. Kenardy, J. Bisson (2009) G. Bonanno, A. Mancini (2010)

major factor in increasing the chances of PTSD, but the reverse is also true. A strong support system can prevent PTSD onset.

Sometimes people diagnosed with PTSD, and people who work with victims, balk at the idea that PTSD is not the normal reaction and is preventable. They feel it is insensitive to the victims, like saying they are weak or mentally inferior in some way. That's not what the scientific research is saying, though. It's research, not a personal attack. The purpose of the research, it should be remembered, is also to help people in the future.

Compare it to cancer research. If there was a study that found a method of preventing cancer that was effective 50 percent of the time, it would be celebrated and promoted. No one would assume that it was being insensitive to people that already have cancer; instead, it would just be great to know that much of the suffering could be prevented in the future.

It's understandable that those victim advocates or critical incident stress responders, because of their sensitivity to victims, don't want to discuss the fact that PTSD is not the normal response and is preventable, but the truth is that really doesn't help future victims. I know that PTSD likely can't be prevented in all cases, but that should not stop us from working toward that goal. There should be a greater focus on resiliency training, not just treatment for those with trouble coping. Isn't it better to prevent somebody from falling, instead of afterward trying to put all the pieces back together again?

We will all face some significant trauma in our lives and will have stress reactions to those events. It is good to know that those reactions are usually temporary and that over the next weeks we will regain a sense of normalcy. The odds are strongly in our favor that we won't develop PTSD. This positive assumption will help us.

If, on the other hand, we assume we will develop PTSD because we experienced a trauma, because we believe that is the most common reaction, it can create a self-fulfilling prophecy. The "placebo effect" is well documented, and it shows that beliefs can help or hinder healing. We need to have a healthy perspective about the natural resiliency of the human mind and our ability to effectively cope with trauma and bounce back.

NATURAL RESILIENCY

The APA states that "a combination of factors contributes to resilience." One of the best ways to learn resiliency is to follow a resilient role model, someone who lives those factors. There are people who have been through every type of stress imaginable and have thrived. Model your behavior (your thoughts, feelings, and actions) after a person who has demonstrated stress resiliency.

It helps to analyze this further to see how having a positive role model has an impact. In Sderot, 44 percent of the children studied had PTSD. But if we break the numbers down further, we find that in families where a parent was suffering from PTSD, their children also had PTSD in 58 percent of the cases. In families where neither parent had PTSD, their children only had it in 28 percent of the cases[7]. So having resilient parents had a large impact on the level of resilience of the children.

7) Source: Israel Center for the Treatment of Psychotrauma.

Not everyone has a resilient role model, of course, and even if you do have one, you may not be able to get down deep into the level of understanding his or her thoughts and feelings. But even without a mentor, you can model the factors that will be covered in the next few chapters.

RESILIENCY FACTORS

There is a growing body of research in the field of resiliency. Resilient people are immune to the negative aspects of stress, have the ability to recover quickly after trauma, and are unlikely to develop PTSD.

Resiliency training is about increasing a person's ability to deal with a high demand without being stressed. Some excellent research on resiliency has been done by the US military, in which they found that the elite Special Forces soldiers had much lower rates of PTSD and other stress issues, despite the greater demands placed on them. When a Navy SEAL is put in some of the most demanding combat situations, he rarely gets PTSD. This scenario was compared with other soldiers who are not placed in similar situations and do have higher rates of PTSD.

Only the most resilient recruits make it through the insanely difficult SEAL training and through the torture of "Hell Week." It makes sense that these "survivors" would be more resilient in battle.

But what is different about these SEALS?

The military research was consistent with the academic

research in leading universities that did similar studies on emotional resilience and mental toughness. The research narrowed it down to some particular traits that these men possess that the less resilient soldiers don't. These characteristics make these individuals immune to the harmful aspects of stress. But the best part of the research is that it demonstrated that these traits, called "resiliency factors," can be learned.

The resiliency factors are thoughts, feelings, or behaviors that research shows make people resilient. Sometimes various researchers use different terminology to describe the factors; however, in order to be consistent I will try to stay away from the academic terminology and use the same names for the factors throughout the book.

The factors are listed here with a short description, and then Part 2 of this book will have a separate chapter for each factor, to describe more fully what it's all about and how you can build it. The factors are not listed in any particular order. There are some factors that overlap or are closely related to other factors. They are listed as separate factors because there are slight distinctions between them that are important to point out.

- Support System – It's important to have trusted friends or a professional therapist to go to.

- Fitness – Stay in shape, exercise, get adequate sleep, and you'll build mental and emotional toughness.

- Body Quieting – Meditate or do breathing exercises to slow your mind and reduce your physiological response to stress.

- Stress-Reduction Diet – Eat the proper foods to keep your body strong and able to fight stress.

- Sense of Humor – Put things in perspective and have the ability to laugh at a situation or at yourself.

- Active Coping Style – Don't avoid your problems; attack them head-on and they will hold less power over you.

- Optimism – Learn to look for the silver lining.

- Finding Meaning in Suffering – The stress you feel is not from the event itself, it's from the meaning you attach to the event.

- Spirituality – Those who believe in a higher power or have a higher purpose for their life are more resilient when facing adversity.

- Self-Confidence, Self-Esteem, and Self-Efficacy – Increase your confidence and self-esteem and you increase your power to deal with negative events.

- Feel in Control – Know that your actions will have an impact on your outcome.

- Stress Inoculation – Build up resistance to stress by exposing yourself to stress in controlled environments.

- Accept Reality – It doesn't do you any good to bury your head in the sand or live in denial.

- Flexibility – Be willing to try different approaches and

roll with the punches.

- Self-Discipline – Exercising self-control strengthens the part of the brain that helps with resilience.

- Creativity – Stimulating our creativity also enhances our ability to cope with stress.

- Live in the Now – Stop living in the past or worrying about the future and you will be more at peace.

- Intelligence – Working to enhance your intelligence has a positive effect on your capacity to handle a high stress load.

- Forgiveness – Practice letting go.

- Love, Compassion, and Gratitude – Altruistic feelings make our life brighter even when bad things happen.

- Perception of Problems – Look at your problems in different and less threatening ways.

The best way to see how these factors work is test them on yourself. Many of these factors may already be a part of your life. Everyone has some resiliency factors as part of their innate personality. Push yourself to implement the factors that you aren't utilizing now and watch for positive benefits. You may connect with one more than another. That's okay. There are many to choose from, but keep in mind that the more you use, the more synergistically they work and the more resilient you become.

Now jump into Part 2 of the book to learn in detail about each one of these factors.

PART TWO
RESILIENCY FACTORS

RESILIENCY FACTOR: A SUPPORT SYSTEM

"When I encourage someone, I see it as an
investment in their resilience."
Steve Karagiannis, author

Having a strong support system with family or your social network is critical for resiliency. According to Dr. Bill McDermott, in his years of practice the biggest problem he saw with cops trying to deal with stress was isolation. We (myself included) typically don't want to open up or share our feelings—perhaps not surprisingly. But we need to have family or friends who we can trust, open up to, and talk about our feelings with.

The first resiliency factor that we will examine is having a support system. The love and care exhibited by trusted family and friends provides a foundation for resiliency. When you are able to lean on them for the support you need, it fosters the healing process; in fact, people who don't have a support system or consider themselves loners often have weaker immune systems. A support system provides the strength and perspective that may be lacking in your life when things are broken. It gives you the power, sometimes by proxy, to take the required steps toward resolving problems, and the power to move toward recovery.

Sometimes it's better to have trusted friends outside of your work environment, creating a less competitive culture. Often you are encouraged to put on a mask in your work environment in order to survive, requiring you to wear a tough façade to avoid having statements like "suck it up, buttercup" or "walk it off, princess" thrown at you. The people delivering these platitudes often mean well, but it obviously discourages honest emotional disclosure. That's why if you are seeking career advancement, you may not want to appear weak by asking for psychological help. I get that. The stigma of mental health issues is being reduced, but don't fool yourself—it's not gone. If you're worried about the stigma at work, then open up and be vulnerable with people who aren't related to your workplace. I also recommend that you establish a support system in addition to your spouse, because if the problem occurs within your marriage you may need some additional help outside of it, such as a marriage counselor, clergy, or good friends.

An additional benefit of having a support system is that it gives you someone to discuss your feelings with versus isolating yourself from everyone. Social isolation can start with just wanting to be alone because of a series of traumatic events in your life. When that withdrawal becomes isolation, however, it can lead to some serious problems such as loneliness, depression, or problems with drugs or alcohol. Research has shown that spending time talking with friends or family can make you feel better and have a positive effect on your health.

According to the US Department of Veterans Affairs, "about six of every ten (or 60 percent) men and five of every ten (or 50 percent) women experience at least one trauma in their lives."[8] This is further complicated for those who have seen combat.

"The number of Veterans with PTSD," the study says, "varies by service era:

- Operations Iraqi Freedom (OIF) and Enduring Freedom (OEF): About 11–20 out of every 100 Veterans (or between 11-20 percent) who served in OIF or OEF have PTSD in a given year.

- Gulf War (Desert Storm): About 12 out of every 100 Gulf War Veterans (or 12 percent) have PTSD in a given year.

- Vietnam War: About 15 out of every 100 Vietnam Veterans (or 15 percent) were diagnosed with PTSD at the time of a study in the late 1980s, the National Vietnam Veterans Readjustment Study (NVVRS). It is estimated that about 30 out of every 100 (or 30 percent) of Vietnam Veterans have had PTSD in their

8) PTSD: National Center for PTSD. (n.d.). Retrieved January 20, 2015, from http://www.ptsd.va.gov/public/PTSD-overview/basics/how-common-is-ptsd.asp.

lifetime."[9]

This gives you a better idea of the percentage of returning veterans that are experiencing PTSD.

Now, to tie those stats to the idea of a support system, let's take a look at the Chris R. Brewin research on the Meta-Analysis of Risk Factors for Posttraumatic Stress Disorder in Trauma-Exposed Adults. In this research, Brewin found that PTSD had little to do with the severity of the trauma and more to do with the support or lack of support received by soldiers after the event.

This finding tends to transcend to the workplace. In workplaces that don't have an adequate social support, people are four times more likely to develop PTSD following trauma. The major variable for resiliency in each of these environments is the professional peer support, or an employee assistance program, and supportive managers who are readily available to help the individual return to as normal a life as possible after the traumatic event. If someone goes through a traumatic experience but has supportive friends and family, or supportive coworkers if it was work-related, they will be less likely to develop PTSD than someone who is isolated.

We can probably all attest to that fact. How often have you been in a stressful incident and noticed that the burden was lighter after having shared the problem with a good friend?

Allow me to illustrate.

In the eleventh grade, my friends and I liked to work out

9) PTSD: National Center for PTSD. (n.d.). Retrieved January 20, 2015, from http://www.ptsd.va.gov/public/PTSD-overview/basics/how-common-is-ptsd.asp.

with weights and do martial arts. I grew up in a small town where the only place to work out was in the school gym; the problem was that it was closed at night. Our solution was to tape over the latch of the emergency door during gym class so we could enter after school hours. Three or four of us would just go in there two or three times a week to work out and put the equipment back when we finished. (As kids, it didn't occur to us that we were breaking the law!)

We didn't have a heavy bag to practice our martial arts with, so one of the things we did was to lay one guy on one of the soft gym mats and simply roll him up in it, almost like a burrito. Then we would tie a skipping rope around him and the gym mat so we could stand him up on his feet, and he would dodge and jump around while the rest of us punched and kicked him, practicing our karate. Simple, but effective!

One day it was my turn to be wrapped up in this mat. My arms were down at my sides with the mat and skipping rope around me so all I could do was jump around as the guys punched at me. Through the window in the hallway, I could see Mr. Alexander, our teacher, walking straight toward the gym. My four friends saw him too, and they ran out of the emergency exit, leaving me standing there alone! I couldn't run anywhere, and I couldn't do anything. I fell over onto my back and tried to squirm my way out of the ridiculous mat, but the rope was tied too tightly. So I was just lying on the floor, looking at the ceiling, wondering, "How am I going to explain this? Am I going to get in trouble or suspended?"

I was feeling stupid and under a high level of stress at this point.

But just then, before Mr. Alexander came in, my friend Dean came running back through the emergency door. He bent down, grabbed me under the arms, and pulled me out of the mat, getting me free. Unfortunately, Mr. Alexander came in just in time to catch us.

The point of this story is this: As soon as Dean came back into the gym, my stress level immediately went way down. It wasn't because I thought we were going to escape or get out of there—Mr. Alexander was too close already. I still knew that I was going to get caught, and I knew that we were going to get into the same trouble I was going to get into before. But there was a difference now: I had a friend there to share it with me. Even though the situation had not changed, the support of a friend made everything easier to bear. (Incidentally, we didn't get into much trouble. Being a gym teacher, Mr. Alexander was impressed with our initiative to work out.)

Even when the reality of a crisis doesn't change, having a support system in place helps your *responses* change. My feelings of stress went down immediately when I saw Dean, even though the nature of the problem had not changed. Your support system is critical to resiliency: having or not having one can make a world of difference.

Chapter Five
Resiliency Factor:
Health and Fitness

"Get comfortable with being uncomfortable!"
Jillian Michaels, expert fitness trainer

According to some experts, health and fitness is the number one resiliency factor. It creates synergy with other factors and has a tremendous impact on agility, endurance, and physical strength.

When you exercise, your body releases those "feel good" biochemicals called endorphins, and regulates the release of three neurotransmitters most commonly associated with the maintenance of mental health: serotonin, norepinephrine, and dopamine. Exercise improves your overall mental picture, and helps flush stress hormones like adrenaline and cortisol from your system. Exercise helps you sleep better, lowers blood pressure, and increases feelings of well-being and self-confidence.

In addition, exercise increases your stamina to deal with a

crisis situation.

Being physically fit to weather the storms of life just makes good common sense. You increase your self-confidence and improve your self-esteem because you are doing something that is good for your body and your mind. When you exercise, BDNF proteins are created in your brain. These proteins are the "fertilizer" for your brain and increase every area of executive function. Exercise also increases your ability to problem solve, and increases your concentration. Dr. John Medina in the book *Brain Rules* says that exercise is as effective as antidepressant medication, and its positive effects start immediately.

It doesn't even have to be much. Depending on your level of health, even walking around the block every day will have a positive impact. Dr. Jeremy Dean says in his article, "Twenty Wonderful Effects Exercise Has on the Mind":

> *Exercise is a powerful antidote to stress, anxiety, and depression. Look for small ways to add activity to your day, like taking the stairs instead of the elevator or going on a short walk. To get the most mental health benefits, aim for thirty minutes or more of exercise per day.*[10]

Dr. Dean lists some additional benefits of exercise, each of which are beneficial for building resiliency:

- Escape a bad mood: If you want to raise your energy

---

10) Dean, J. (n.d.). 20 Wonderful Effects Exercise Has on the Mind. Retrieved January 20, 2015, from http://www. spring.org.uk/2013/10/20-wonderful-effects-exercise-has-on-the-mind.php.

levels, reduce tension, and boost mood, you can talk to your friends or listen to some music. But most agree that for the difficult job of transforming a bad mood into a good one, exercise is the most effective method (Thayer et al., 1994).

- Fight depression: Just as exercise fights anxiety, it also fights its close relation, depression. One review of thirty-nine different studies involving 2,326 people has found that exercise generally provides moderate relief from depression (Cooney et al., 2013). The effects may be as great as starting therapy or taking antidepressants.

- Reduces anxiety: Exercise has a relatively long-lasting protective effect against anxiety (Smith, 2013). Both low- and medium-intensity exercise have been shown to reduce anxiety. However, those doing high-intensity exercise are likely to experience the greatest reduction in anxiety, especially among women (Cox et al., 2004).

- Speed up your mind: Working memory includes what's in your conscious mind right now and whatever you're doing with this information. After thirty minutes [of] exercise, people's working memory improves. There's some evidence that accuracy drops a bit, but this is more than made up for by increases in speed (McMorris et al., 2011).

- Boost self-control: A review of twenty-four different studies on the effects of exercise on self-control found that a short bout provides an immediate boost to self-control (Verburgh et al., 2013). Although regular exercise didn't show an effect on self-control, a period of moderate exercise did allow people to take better control of themselves.

- Help with serious mental disorders: Schizophrenia is a serious mental disorder often involving hallucinations, paranoia, and confused thinking. Despite its severe nature, there's evidence that exercise can help for this, as well as alcoholism and body image disorder (Tkachuk et al., 1999).

- Stimulate brain cell growth: Part of the reason that exercise is beneficial in so many different mental areas is that it helps new brain cells to grow. A study on rats has shown that, in response to exercise, the brain regions related to memory and learning grow (Bjørnebekk, 2007).

- Increase executive functioning: What psychologists call "executive functioning" includes all kinds of useful abilities like being able to switch tasks efficiently, ignore distractions, make plans, and so on. Reviewing many studies in this area, Guiney and Machado (2012) find that exercise reliably improves executive function, especially in older adults.[11]

In addition to all these great benefits, physical exercise also

11) IDean, J. (n.d.). 20 Wonderful Effects Exercise Has on the Mind. Retrieved January 20, 2015, from http://www.spring.org.uk/2013/10/20-wonderful-effects-exercise-has-on-the-mind.php.

promotes a more restful sleep. It helps the release of tension and promotes muscle relaxation. People who exercise sleep more soundly than those who are not active, especially when under stress. A study of over seven thousand adults at Brigham Young University showed that while adults who exercise have the same number of demands and pressures as those who don't, exercisers perceive significantly fewer problems in their lives. Despite stressful circumstances, exercise brings a more positive outlook.

SLEEP'S EFFECT ON RESILIENCY

When studying resiliency, researchers tend to examine exercise and nutrition instead of sleep. But according to the Resilience Institute, "Steadily growing evidence finds sleep to be a key factor in preventable disease, distress, well-being, emotional competence, and cognition."[12]

Sleep has been something that North Americans have taken for granted for centuries. It's also often been equated to laziness, and no one wants to be considered lazy. Jerry Seinfeld summed up the typical American's plight pretty nicely when he said, "We want to do a lot of stuff. We're not in great shape. We didn't get a good night's sleep. We're a little depressed. Coffee solves all these problems in one delightful little cup."

But a cup of coffee is only a temporary fix to a systemic problem. We work long days and binge-watch Netflix and surf the web late into the night. Our electronic devices are available

---

12) Resilience Insight: Sleep Salvation. (n.d.). Retrieved January 21, 2015, from http://www.resiliencei.com/articles/Health/5/127/Resilience-Insight-Sleep-Salvation.

24/7, and we can't make a move without them, even to sleep. Sleep deficiency is often undetectable because its symptoms are closely related to other infirmities.

So what does this have to do with resiliency?

A lot. Experts tell us that we need seven to eight hours of sleep per night, making sleep as important as exercise and nutrition or more as you return to normalcy after a traumatic situation. Your "body clock," or biological clock, determines which time of the day is appropriate for sleeping. When our bodies are denied sleep even for a short amount of time, it can cause a health-related tsunami such as hunger, craving, memory loss, and infertility. If our body clock is disrupted on a regular basis, it could lead to a fatal illness such as cancer, diabetes, or heart disease.

Our sleep is governed by the ultradian rhythm in 90- to 110-minute intervals. The first two cycles are deep sleep, the next three are REM. Anxiety, depression, sleep apnea, and medication can disturb this cycle and compromise hormonal function and resilience.

Getting the right amount of sleep at the right time should be a priority and will assist you in building a lifestyle that improves your overall quality of life. Here are some tips to help you successfully fulfill your mission:

- Attempt to get at least seven and a half hours of sleep per night.

- Avoid all technology for at least two hours before bedtime.

- Your bedroom should be cool, dark, and quiet.
- A power nap in the middle of the day sustains productivity.

THE NUMBER ONE FACTOR

If I am forced to pick just one factor as the most important for building stress immunity, I always say health and fitness.

Working out and getting enough sleep provides obvious benefits to physical health, such as increased stamina, endurance, and physical strength, which help you get through critical events…but the benefits go way beyond that. Had a bad day at work? Have a sick feeling in your stomach from all the stress hormones in your system? Go for a run! Nothing will make you feel better—at least nothing without harmful side effects!

Personally, when I get angry about something at work, the most effective way for me to get rid of it is to go for a 5k run. I usually go at a faster pace when I'm mad, but after a mile or two I've burned it right out of me, and I feel good. I feel relaxed and confident and able to let go of whatever was bothering me.

No worries—you don't have to be a marathon runner. Start wherever you can, but get active, watch your need for rest, and reap the rewards.

CHAPTER SIX

RESILIENCY FACTOR: BODY QUIETING

*"I can be stressed, or tired, and I can go into a
meditation and it all just flows off of me. I'll come out
of it refreshed and centered, and that's how I'll feel
and it'll carry through the day."*
Ray Dalio, founder of the world's largest hedge fund

"Body quieting" is a term used to describe various techniques used for slowing down your mind and body, such as meditation, yoga, and breathing techniques, among others. Researchers have found a vast amount of wealth in body quieting and its benefits in regards to being resilient. There is a need to quiet the body and the mind. Many studies on meditation show that people who meditate react better in stressful circumstances.

You may think this is one of those California, New Age, "woo woo" things, but it's not. Hear me out. People who meditate or do some type of body quieting on a daily basis experience physical changes in their body: their adrenal glands secrete less adrenaline and cortisol when stressed, and they have access to better judgment and better problem-solving skills under stress.

I spoke to a friend a while back who spent nine days in silence at a retreat, meditating all day. I thought that was awesome, if you can afford the time to do that. However, it may not be realistic for most of us to take nine days away from family or career (or Facebook!). Fortunately, you don't need to do that to start seeing benefits. Start with a short time. I take ten minutes at work to close my office door and meditate, listening to Solitudes music or *Deepak Chopra: Soul of Healing Affirmations* that I downloaded from iTunes. Taking that mere ten minutes has a huge positive impact on the rest of my day. It reduces stress instantly and gives perspective to whatever else I have going on.

But there are even easier methods. I've incorporated a breathing technique in this chapter, which is a quick and effective way to quiet your body and mind.

TACTICAL BREATHING

Tactical breathing can be used to immediately reduce stress. It has an impact physically and psychologically.

David Grossman, a Lieutenant Colonel (Retired) in the US Army Rangers and a psychologist, teaches cops and soldiers how to do tactical breathing in his book, *On Combat: The*

Psychology and Physiology of Deadly Conflict in War and Peace.
You start by breathing from your diaphragm. As you breathe
in your stomach expands, and it contracts as you breathe out.
(Tip: Think of your stomach as a balloon filling with air as you
breathe in and emptying smoothly and automatically as you
breathe out.)

- Breathe in through your nose to the count of four.

- Hold your breath to the count of four.

- Breathe out through your lips to the count of four.

- Hold your breath to the count of four.

- Repeat three or four times.

You can use tactical breathing when you are actively dealing
with a stressful or traumatic situation to help control your
mind and your body's stress reaction. You can also do it after a
stressful event to return to a normal state.

It really is that simple.

MEDITATION

People have told me that they want to read and educate
themselves about meditation. However, when they begin
to learn about the different types, such as transcendental,
mindfulness, guided visualization, Japa, etc., it suddenly seems
big and complicated.

I understand, because I did the same thing. I bought three
books on meditation before I even tried doing it. I realized

eventually that all that wasn't necessary, or the best way to begin. It's better to keep it simple at the start. Just sit still, quiet your mind, quiet your body, and you're doing meditation.

As thoughts come into your mind, allow them to pass… watch them go. Refocus on your breathing. Or focus on the present moment. Exercise discipline on your mind by bringing it back to the present moment if your thoughts begin to wander to the past or future. That's harder than it sounds since our mind is occupied with past and future most of the time. Another method is to say an affirmation or mantra over and over in your mind, or focus on an emotion such as gratitude or compassion. Feel it.

It's not so much about what kind of meditation you do, but that you do it. It's about creating the habit. I know there are a lot of techniques, and it can be overwhelming. But just pick one that sounds appealing and *start*. The regular practice of meditation is what will bring benefits into all aspects of your life: mental, physical, spiritual, and emotional. Learning to quiet your mind and body and just be in the present moment will reduce feelings of stress and also reduce the physical reactions to stress.

The purpose of meditation is to increase our awareness and improve our perception of our challenges or painful experiences. It will enhance your immune function and helps to regulate brain chemicals, as well. Basically, meditation brings peace into your life.

But not by simply reading about it. *Try it*.

OTHER TECHNIQUES

Some other effective techniques to implement in your body quieting plan of action are:

- Breathing techniques: Therapeutic exercises aimed to deepen inspiration or expiration or even to alter the rate and rhythm of respiration.[13]

- Massage: Group of systematic and scientific manipulations of body tissues best performed with the hands for the purpose of affecting the nervous and muscular systems and the general circulation.[14]

- Reiki: Placing the healer's hands upon the person to be cured with the intent of spiritual energetic healing.[15]

- Visualization: Helps you imagine yourself being in a particular state of relaxation.

- Progressive relaxation: Developed in 1909 by E. Jacobson at Harvard, and used in mind-body medicine to cope with stress, in which muscle groups are flexed in succession, starting at one end of the body and going to the other.[16]

- Self-hypnosis: The process of putting oneself into a trancelike state by autosuggestion, such as concentration on a single thought or object. Some subjects are more

---

13) Medical Concept Reference Encyclopedia. (n.d.). Retrieved January 20, 2015, from http://www.reference.md.
14) Ibid.
15) Ibid.
16) Progressive relaxation. (n.d.) Segen's Medical Dictionary. (2011). Retrieved January 20 2015 from http://medical-dictionary.thefreedictionary.com/progressive+relaxation.

susceptible than others.[17]

- Yoga: The term comes from a Sanskrit word which means yoke or union. Traditionally, yoga is a method of joining the individual self with the Divine, Universal Spirit, or Cosmic Consciousness. Physical and mental exercises are designed to help achieve this goal, also called self-transcendence or enlightenment. On the physical level, yoga postures, called *asanas*, are designed to tone, strengthen, and align the body. These postures are performed to make the spine supple and healthy and to promote blood flow to all the organs, glands, and tissues, keeping all the bodily systems healthy. On the mental level, yoga uses breathing techniques (*pranayama*) and meditation (*dyana*) to quiet, clarify, and discipline the mind. However, experts are quick to point out that yoga is not a religion, but a way of living with health and peace of mind as its aims.[18]

- Prayer: Communication with the spiritual or "ultimate" reality, which may be understood as transcendent or immanent, and described in theistic or nontheistic terms.[19]

Not all body quieting techniques will resonate with you. That's ok. Pick one, and work on it. When you are stressed or

17) Self-hypnosis. (n.d.) Mosby's Medical Dictionary, 8th edition. (2009). Retrieved January 20 2015 from http://medical-dictionary.thefreedictionary.com/self-hypnosis.
18) Yoga. (n.d.) Gale Encyclopedia of Medicine. (2008). Retrieved January 20 2015 from http://medical-dictionary.thefreedictionary.com/Yoga.
19) Prayer. (n.d.) Segen's Medical Dictionary. (2011). Retrieved January 20 2015 from http://medical-dictionary.thefreedictionary.com/Prayer.

overwhelmed at work you may feel like you don't even have time to take a three-minute break, but that is when you need it the most. Stop what you are doing. Close your eyes and do a breathing or progressive relaxation technique. You will be less stressed and more effective with your work afterwards.

CHAPTER SEVEN

RESILIENCY FACTOR:
STRESS-REDUCTION DIET

"Never go to excess, but let moderation be your guide."
Marcus Tullius Cicero

People often go on diets as a tactic to lose weight, but eating healthier meals and snacks can also help build your resiliency. Did you know that certain foods promote stress reduction? We will take a look at them later in this chapter.

When going through a stressful time, some of us tend not to eat while others eat too much. One of the things we need to do is regulate both our eating and sleeping; we need to resume normalcy as quickly as possible. Getting the physiological aspects of our life back in sync helps with the emotional side.

EFFECTS OF AN IMPROPER
DIET DURING STRESS

Poor nutrition and bad eating habits can compromise

performance, stamina, and stress tolerance. I'm not going to get into a whole lesson on nutrition here, because numerous dieticians out there can point you in the right direction. I'll just mention some of the big-picture diet items that can help or hurt us. A couple of the common addictions in the typical American diet are caffeine and sugar. Caffeine and sugar are both adrenaline enhancers, which add to high stress levels, nervousness, and irritability. (Granted, I wouldn't have been able to write this book if it wasn't for caffeine, so it does have its uses! Just keep in mind that it will enhance stress and keep your stress levels elevated for longer periods.)

Alcohol is a depressant and interrupts regular sleep routines, suppressing REM sleep. It also reduces levels of vitamin B and C that are needed for the body to deal with stress. So although alcohol can feel like a good way to deal with stress in the short term, on a long-term basis it is counterproductive. Alcohol also *increases* production of cortisol and *decreases* testosterone.[20] That's a double whammy because cortisol is a stress hormone, and testosterone is a hormone (which both men and women have to different degrees) that enhances our ability to deal with stress.

Sometimes in the hustle and bustle of everyday life, we make eating healthy our last priority. You must be intentional in planning your meals and exercise around your work and play schedule, especially if you work in a demanding, stressful environment. Remember, work-life balance and good health contributes to your being resilient when the chips are down. The sooner you can get back to normal, the more likely you

---

20) King, B. (2012) The Ultimate Male Solution (pp. 114-115) Abundant Health Systems.

will bounce back faster. Having a routine in place to get back to helps you psychologically.

I've seen people I work with (and I've done it myself) use copious amounts of coffee to get through long shifts. With the younger generation it's often Red Bull instead of coffee. Either way, it keeps stress hormones elevated. Then at the end of the shift it's alcohol to bring themselves down. Research shows that in moderate amounts both are ok. I'm with Dr. Oz on that. But when alcohol is used as a crutch to deal with stress or avoid pain in life, then it's harmful.

BENEFITS OF A PROPER DIET DURING STRESS

A healthy diet, on the other hand, helps your body deal with the physiological aspects of stress.

Eating a diet high in phytonutrients and antioxidants (from fresh fruits and vegetables, mostly) will help your body fight stress. Vitamin B, magnesium, and omega-3 fatty acids can be used as stress supplements. They've all been shown to protect the body against the physiological aspects of stress. Research also shows that healthy bacteria (probiotics) found in bio-active yogurt or as a supplement can actually improve mood. An inharmonious environment in the gut can cause issues that wreak havoc on your moods.

Realize that the healthy food that you eat is a direct remedy for the stress you may be experiencing in your life. In WebMD's "Foods that Help Tame Stress" article, it is stated that:

Foods can help tame stress in several ways. Comfort foods, like a bowl of warm oatmeal, boost levels of serotonin, a calming brain chemical. Other foods can cut levels of cortisol and adrenaline, stress hormones that take a toll on the body over time. A healthy diet can help counter the impact of stress by shoring up the immune system and lowering blood pressure.[21]

The article lists the following foods as stress tamers:

- Complex Carbs – They prompt the brain to make more serotonin and help you feel balanced by stabilizing your blood sugar levels. An example of a complex carb is oatmeal.

- Simple Carbs – In an emergency situation, a small amount is good. They digest quickly, leading to a spike in serotonin. This doesn't last long, so remember moderation is the key to using this stress buster. An example of a simple carb is fruit.

- Oranges – They are packed with vitamin C that can curb levels of stress hormones while strengthening the immune system.

- Spinach – This stress buster is chock-full of magnesium, which may suppress headaches and fatigue that often compound stress.

21) Diet for Stress Management Slideshow: Carbs, Nuts, and Other Stress-Relief Foods. (n.d.). Retrieved January 20, 2015, from http://www.webmd.com/diet/ss/slideshow-diet-for-stress-management.

- Fatty Fish – Yes, fatty fish such as salmon and tuna have omega-3 fatty acids, which can prevent surges in stress hormones. They also may help protect you against heart disease, depression, and PMS.

- Green Tea – Drinking green tea may cause you to have lower levels of the stress hormone cortisol after experiencing a stressful situation, and green tea is an excellent antioxidant.

- Pistachios – The healthy fats in this stress buster lower your cholesterol, ease inflammation in your heart's arteries, make diabetes less likely, and protect you against the effects of stress.

- Avocados – This stress buster helps you reduce high blood pressure because it is loaded with potassium, plus it has healthy fats that are good for your brain.

- Almonds – Almonds contain vitamin E to bolster your immune system and vitamin B that helps you be more resilient during bouts with depression.

- Bedtime Snack – A small amount of carbs at bedtime can speed the release of the brain chemical serotonin and help you sleep better.

- Herbal Supplements – There are numerous herbal supplements that claim to fight stress, such as St. John's wort and valerian root. They both have been reported to have a calming effect on their users.[22]

---

22) Diet for Stress Management Slideshow: Carbs, Nuts, and Other Stress-Relief Foods. (n.d.). Retrieved January 20, 2015, from http://www.webmd.com/diet/ss/slideshow-diet-for-stress-management.

All of these foods can help you build resiliency. Again, remember to use substances like alcohol, sugar and caffeine in moderation, combined with a healthy diet and you will be well on your way to a healthy body, mind, and spirit.

Good food is one of those factors, I find, that fitness works with synergistically. Whenever I'm on my exercise routine I eat healthier and sleep better. When I stop exercising, then I don't care as much about what I put into my body.

CHAPTER EIGHT
RESILIENCY FACTOR: A SENSE OF HUMOR

"Good humor is a tonic for mind and body. It is the best antidote for anxiety and depression. It is a business asset. It attracts and keeps friends. It lightens human burdens. It is the direct route to serenity and contentment."
Grenville Kleiser – 1868-1935, author

Humor allows you to get a different perspective on what has happened to you in life. It allows you to step back from a situation and view it differently, and you can examine it from far enough away that it doesn't reach out and pull you into the past. Laughter puts a pretty face on an ugly event or circumstance. What held you captive to negative emotions can finally become something you can accept.

Drs. Steven J. Wolin and Sybil Wolin wrote a book entitled *The Resilient Self*, in which they say humor, along with creativity, "turn[s] nothing into something and something into nothing."[23] Not taking ourselves too seriously can be a shield that protects us from stress.

Laughter, it is well known, is good medicine for the soul. It's hard to feel self-pity when you're in the middle of busting your gut in laughter! Standup comedians say that the equation is "Tragedy + time = comedy." Humor has a positive biological effect on the body, as well. "Humor has been identified as an important coping mechanism that reduces the threatening nature of stressful situations" (Martin 2003). Laughter not only works well for major stressors but also for everyday stressors, often called "first-world problems." Check out First-World-Problems.com to see what I mean. People tweet and post things that are stressing them out or pet peeves that get them angry. However much they may frustrate us in the moment, some of the things that stress us in North America in this decade you just have to chill out and laugh at.

Some of my favorite examples:

- My Wifi just went down for 1 hour.

- My poodle can't get a haircut today because of the humidity outside…ugh, so annoyed with stupid global warming!

- Uggggh! I just got the iPhone 5s and they just announced the release of the 6 next month! Now I have to go back to Verizon and wait in line again.

- I have too much chips for my dip, but if I open more dip, I'll have too much dip for my chips.

---

23) Humor. (n.d.). Retrieved January 21, 2015, from http://www.pbs.org/thisemotionallife/topic/humor/humor-and-resilience.

- Wife bought me a Google Chrome Cast, now I have more HDMI devices than I have HDMI inputs.

- Asked for no whip cream on my Tall Starbucks order, they gave me a Grande with *extra* whip cream!

The humor in situations like these may be obvious to us, but we can laugh at more serious stressors, too. Being able to laugh during tragic circumstances has a protective effect. It gives you a different set of glasses with which to view your trial. Sometimes, of course, there are tragic circumstances that aren't appropriate to laugh at; however, the more we can find to laugh at, the more protective effect this attitude will have on our psyche.

Medical and law enforcement personnel deal with trauma every day. Nurses, doctors, and those in emergency services need the ability to laugh about trauma at the appropriate times— not to be callous or cruel, but to protect their psyches and allow them to continue doing their duties well and efficiently. Too much empathy when you are dealing with tragic circumstances every day can cause Secondary Traumatic Stress (STS).

An early study of this showed that Vietnam veterans who had a good sense of humor, despite the trauma they experienced, had lower rates of PTSD. When all else was out of their control, humor was one of the few things that remained. In *Man's Search for Meaning*, psychiatrist Victor Frankl wrote about his experience in Nazi concentration camps. Humor, he said,

...was another of the soul's weapons in the fight for self-preservation. It is well known that humor, more than anything else in the human makeup, can afford an aloofness and an ability to rise above any situation, even if only for a few seconds.

Linda Graham had this to say about the health benefits of laughter:

Laughter triggers catecholamines in the brain that heighten alertness. Laughter releases endorphins, the body's natural pain killer. Laughter cleanses the body of the stress hormone cortisol, lowering blood pressure, reducing stress and increasing pain tolerance. Laughter's alternating contraction-relaxation of the diaphragm releases tension in the body, bringing our autonomic nervous system into balance. (The physiological effects of a good session of laughter can last up to 45 minutes.)

Laughter increases the flow of blood and oxygen through our coronary arteries, reducing the risk of heart disease and stroke. Laughter staves off the anxiety and depression that can severely impact heart functioning. Laughter mitigates the damaging effects of inflammation, reducing the pain of arthritis. Laughter strengthens the immune system, helping the body fight off viruses and cancer. Laughter helps stabilize blood sugar levels in diabetics. Laughter improves respiratory functioning in patients with chronic lung disease. Laughter even burns calories.[24]

Can you look back on misfortunes or challenges in your past and laugh about them? Okay, well, that's pretty easy. How about finding the humor in your present difficulties? That's a lot harder. But it's also healthier.

People who can find humor in their problems, who can laugh at themselves and who don't take themselves too seriously, are simply more resilient. They can bounce back from traumas and deal with everyday stresses much more easily.

When I was team leader for a police tactical unit in Northern Ontario, we had a guy who could always crack us up. No matter how cold, wet, and tired we were, no matter how miserable the situation was, Ryan could always find something funny about it. He was relentless with the jokes. Although it didn't seem like a critical skill in those emergency situations, I considered him a critical player on our team. Why? Because I knew that no matter how bad things got, morale wouldn't spiral downward and team members wouldn't be overwhelmed by the demanding situation because he would have them laughing.

Laughing feels good, and it's good for you. What has you stressed, frustrated, angry, or overwhelmed? What can you find *right now* that is funny about it?

It's not always easy, I know...but it *works*.

---

24) Graham, L. (n.d.). Laughter. Retrieved January 21, 2015, from http://lindagraham-mft.net/resources/published-articles/laughter/.

CHAPTER NINE

RESILIENCY FACTOR: AN ACTIVE COPING STYLE

"The only way around is through…"
Robert Frost

The paths that we travel on are often strewn with obstacles. Hitting these obstacles in life can slow us down and keep us from making progress. Having a fighting spirit to go around, over, or through the obstacle, however, is an "active coping style" and helps us achieve success. This is one more protective factor that can reduce the chance of negative effects of stress.

An active coping style is basically the opposite of avoidance. You attack the problem head-on instead of burying your head in the sand. You actually take the position of a victor versus that of a victim, and in that very moment implement a problem-solving strategy. You make a specific behavioral and psychological effort to master or minimize stressful events that happen in your life.

Dr. Glenn Schiraldi, in his book *The Complete Guide to Resilience*, gives a helpful list to define what active copers are:

- They are proactive doers and problem solvers. That is, they are engaged in life. They anticipate and prepare for difficulties, rather than waiting for crises to strike. They appraise situations and take reasonable action, learning and applying needed skills.

- They are adventurous. Adventurous means disposed to cope with the new and unknown.

- They are curious. Curious people don't get down during stress, but approach problems with pleasant and engaged interest.

- They acknowledge that a problem exists. They think about it, generate and weigh alternative solutions, make and follow a plan of action, and have a back-up plan.

- They are conscientious. That is, they work hard, are determined to build a better life, [and] want to improve, persist, and make use of needed resources.

- They are disciplined. They organize—creating structure, order, and routine. They follow through with their plans. They train themselves to forego immediate pleasures and destructive shortcuts in the pursuit of a long-term goal. They act despite difficulties, fears, and risks.

- They keep dreams and make goals. These goals are guided by internal core values, not the dictates of others.

- They focus on "what's the most important thing to do right now to get me closer to my goal?"

These principles are the basics of how to engage in an active coping lifestyle and create a life of growing resiliency.

There are generally two types of strategies for dealing with stressors in your life: one is *problem-solving* and the other is *emotion-focused*. Problem-solving strategies involve you doing something *actively* to alleviate your problem. For example, if debt is causing you stress, you personally choose a means or create an action plan to alleviate the problem. You take steps to get your finances in order and eliminate the debt, like setting up an automatic payment plan and creating a budget.

Emotion-focused strategies involve your attempt to regulate your emotional response to a difficult situation. For example, you may have just been diagnosed with an illness. An emotion-focused strategy is not about curing the illness, but about handling our emotions. A person may meditate or look for a meaning or purpose in the suffering to be able to handle the stress.

Let's visit stress and active coping styles from the perspective of an article by author Şerife Terzi in *The Journal of Happiness and Well-Being* that looks at coping with stress and resilience among university students:

Lazarus and Folkman define stress as a transaction between the person and the environment, in which the individual considers that the environmental demands outweigh their ability to meet those demands. Coping is defined as "constantly changing cognitive and behavioral effort to manage specific external and internal demands that are appraised as taxing or exceeding the resources of the person." Folkman and Lazarus suggested two types of coping that they labeled emotion-focused and problem-focused.[25]

People that use both problem-solving strategies *and* emotion-focused strategies to deal with stress are the best active copers. Who are those people? They are those that possess a "fighting spirit," people that love a challenge, and those that seem to thrive on chaos.

You must face your problems and deal with them as opposed to dodging, denying, or totally disengaging from your reality.

Let me share an example of someone who did *not* use an active coping style, choosing denial and avoidance instead.

Gary is a friend of mine, a sergeant in the same police department. Back when he was in the fourth grade, he was stressed about having to give a speech in front of his class. Instead of dealing with the stress, he faked sickness on the day of his speech. Because the speeches lasted for a few days to get everyone finished, he knew if he went back the next day he

25) Terzi, S. (2013). Secure attachment style, coping with stress and resilience among university students. *The Journal of Happiness and Well-Being, 1*(2), 99-99. Retrieved January 21, 2015, from http://journalofhappiness.net/pdf/v01i02/v01-i02-06.pdf.

would still have to do his speech, so he kept faking stomach pain for the whole week. His mother took him to the doctor a couple of times that week, and they couldn't figure out what the pain was from. The only diagnosis the doctor could render was that he had appendicitis. So Gary was taken in for surgery and had his perfectly healthy appendix removed! He was nine at the time, and figured surgery and recovery were better than making that speech. He was off from school for a month recovering…and when he got back to school, the teacher made him do the speech.

Dr. Phil would ask him, "And how's that working for ya?"

Denial and avoidance don't work.

An example where I used an active coping style happened about sixteen years ago. At the time I was part of a Police Emergency Response Team, similar to what you might think of as a SWAT Team. We covered a large area of remote territory. A plane carrying some hunters crashed in an isolated area, and my team was sent to cut a trail in through the bush and retrieve the bodies. There were body parts strewn about the crash site. There were some body parts inside what was left of the fuselage; those had been cooked from the fire that burned after the crash. We had to pick up the pieces to place in body bags. At one point, I picked up a man's thigh. There were no clothes left on it, and the way the fat and muscle were cooked, it reminded me of a ham. After that I couldn't eat ham for a couple of years. Just to see a cooked ham made me nauseous.

That nausea was a traumatic stress reaction, but it wasn't PTSD. It was just one symptom. I knew I didn't want to live like that, though, because I used to like ham. So in order to actively cope with the stressor, I forced myself to eat ham at Christmas or Easter or whenever my family was serving it. And it was awful at first. I didn't enjoy it. It made me feel sick. However, over time I was able to associate the taste and smell of ham to the holidays and not to trauma. My forced-ham-eating therapy worked, and I can tell you now that I really enjoy a honey-baked ham with some Dijon mustard and scalloped potatoes. The aroma of ham reminds me of family celebrations. I'm getting hungry right now, thinking about it. It was a problem-solving strategy that helped me change the subconscious association I had to ham. It didn't happen on its own, though. I had to act! I had to expose myself to what disturbed me, and had to stop my avoidance behaviors.

My personal example is a highly graphic one, perhaps, but I use it to demonstrate just one way that an active coping style works. You likely won't ever experience what I experienced in this case, but you can certainly benefit from these methods to recover from smaller—or even greater—trauma. Have the grit to face your demons and find solutions.

CHAPTER TEN
RESILIENCY FACTOR:
OPTIMISM

"We can always choose to perceive things differently.
We can focus on what's wrong in our life,
or we can focus on what's right."
Marianne Williamson, author

Being an optimistic, hopeful person decreases stress. Dr. Martin Seligman's research shows that optimism can be learned. Optimism doesn't mean letting your guard down, believing everyone loves you, or that no one will hurt you. Optimism is an attitude of seeing the silver lining, as opposed to negativity and cynicism. It's about hope for the future, about knowing there is more good than bad in the world. It's knowing that you as an individual can make a difference in your outcome. It's knowing that negative events in your life are temporary and you will be able to overcome them.

OPTIMISM VERSUS
CYNICISM AND PESSIMISM

Optimism is when a person has hope in the future or expects a positive result in a particular situation. *Realistic* optimism is accepting the difficult truth of a situation, as opposed to being idealistic or a Pollyanna, but still believing you will succeed in the end. An optimistic person accepts the hand that they were dealt, acknowledges reality, and has faith that eventually everything will work out for their good.

Facing the Nazi threat, Winston Churchill spoke on May 13, 1940 to the House of Commons. He stated:

> *I would say to the House, as I said to those who have joined this Government; I have nothing to offer but blood, toil, tears, and sweat. We have before us an ordeal of the most grievous kind. We have before us many, many long months of struggle and of suffering. You ask what is our policy? I will say: It is to wage war, by sea, land, and air, with all our might and with all our strength that God can give us... That is our policy. You ask, What is our aim? I can answer in one word: Victory—victory at all costs, victory in spite of all terror; victory, however long and hard the road may be.*

Churchill is an example of a leader who demonstrated realistic optimism. He didn't demonstrate pessimism and give up, thinking all was lost. Nor did he demonstrate Pollyanna optimism, by saying "Don't worry, no big deal. We're on an island, we'll be just fine!" He had the right level of realistic optimism. He recognized the serious threat, he knew the situation England was in, yet he still had faith that they would prevail in the end. He knew ultimate victory was theirs, whatever the cost.

Realistic optimism is a belief system that helps people actively cope, because on one hand they don't believe that there is no hope, and on the other, they are not Pollyanna believing that everything will be fine without them taking the necessary action.

Cynicism, by contrast, is when a person is inclined to believe that people are motivated purely by self-interest. They are suspicious about everyone's motives and use this perception as their measuring stick for everything. Pessimism, further, is when a person has a negative perspective on life, lacking hope in the future. They are usually contaminated with doubt and unbelief, and often struggle to derive joy from things around them.

BENEFITS OF OPTIMISM

Hundreds of studies have shown the impact of being an optimist or a pessimist. For example, optimists tend to:

- Do much better in school
- Exceed the predictions of aptitude tests
- Have greater success when they run for office

- Show greater persistence when looking to achieve goals
- Age better
- Usually experience better health, and
- May even live longer.

STOCKDALE PARADOX,
THE MISINTERPRETATION

In the book *Good to Great*, author Jim Collins features Admiral Jim Stockdale. General Stockdale was the highest-ranking US military officer in the "Hanoi Hilton" prisoner-of-war camp during the Vietnam War. Here is a snapshot of Collins's conversation with General Stockdale after his release:

I [Collins] asked, "Who didn't make it out?"

"Oh, that's easy," he [General Stockdale] said. "The optimists."

"The optimists? I don't understand," I said.

"The optimists. Oh, they were the ones who said, 'We're going to be out by Christmas.' And Christmas would come, and Christmas would go. Then they'd say, 'We're going to be out by Easter.' And Easter would come, and Easter would go. And then Thanksgiving, and then it would be Christmas again. And they died of a broken heart."

[After] another long pause, he turned to me and said, "This is a very important lesson. You must never confuse faith that you will prevail in the end—which you can never afford to lose— with the discipline to confront the most brutal facts of your current reality, whatever they might be."[26]

Upon first glance, it appears as though General Stockdale was implying that optimists don't have staying power in tough situations. On the contrary, he was referring to the type of optimism that better fits the definition of "Pollyanna optimism," which is often used as *an escape from the reality of a situation while embracing a falsehood.*

The emotions of these POWs could easily be misinterpreted as optimism because of how it appeared on the surface. But it was not a real optimism; it was actually Pollyanna optimism because there was no real *basis* for their feelings, no *realistic* evaluation of their situation. Again, realistic optimism is when people are willing to face the truth. They accept the *reality* of the situation, but still have *faith* and hope. Their attitude, rather than "We're getting of here by Christmas," would be "We're going to get out of here in the long run." It doesn't sound as encouraging as the former, perhaps, but they do not have a deluded, unrealistic sense of optimism. The former were originally overly optimistic, but then what happened? They became pessimistic, and eventually they lost all faith. Realistic

26) Collins, J. (2001). The Stockdale Paradox. In *Good to Great: Why some companies make the leap—and others don't* (pp. 83 - 85). New York, NY: HarperBusiness.

optimists keep touch with reality, but have an underlying faith that they will prevail.

Research shows that optimists survive traumatic experiences better than others, and the reasons become clear as we look closer at the defining characteristics of optimists. Realistic optimism prompts action. Pessimists tend to give up, thinking there is no hope. They have a victim attitude. Because they give up, they do not have an active coping style. Pollyanna optimists don't take action either, for a completely different reason. They believe that it will all just work out. So they tend to not be active copers and fighters either.

My advice is to always confront reality and stay positive. General Stockdale was a key catalyst in developing survival strategies that kept his men alive during the war. He honestly confronted reality, stayed positive, and taught his men how to do likewise. These men learned how to be optimistic while facing the reality of their difficulties.

So, what if you're "naturally" a pessimist or prone to unrealistic optimism? Can you learn to face reality better and still maintain a healthy, positive attitude?

Absolutely.

THREE DIMENSIONS
OF HABITUAL THINKING

Dr. Martin Seligman, a famous psychologist, said in his book, *Learned Optimism*, that "Optimism is invaluable for the meaningful life. With a firm belief in a positive future, you can throw yourself into the service of that which is larger than you are."

The level of optimism that you possess, like many aspects of resiliency, is based on how your worldview was formed as a child. Optimism, though, *can* be learned and is another key component to resiliency. You have a choice between optimism, pessimism, and cynicism. And it *is* a *choice*.

Seligman goes on to suggest that positive psychology can be taught to combat negative self-talk and pessimistic thinking. "The basis of optimism," Seligman suggests, "does not lie in positive phrases or images of victory, but in the way you think about causes."[27] In defining optimists, he states that,

> *The optimists, who are confronted with the same hard knocks...tend to believe defeat is just a temporary setback, that its causes are confined to this one case. The optimists believe defeat is not entirely their fault: Circumstances, bad luck, or other people brought it about. Such people are unfazed by defeat. Confronted by a bad situation, they perceive it as a challenge and try harder.[28]*

> *In his discussion on learned optimism, he states that,*

> *Learned optimism is not a rediscovery of the 'power of positive thinking.' The skills of optimism do not emerge from the pink Sunday-school world*

27) Positive Psychology Resources, Optimism, Overview. (n.d.). Retrieved January 22, 2015, from http://www.centre-forconfidence.co.uk/pp/overview.php?p=c2lkPTQmdGlkPTAmaWQ9NTU=.
28) Seligman, M. (1991). Learned optimism. New York: A.A. Knopf.

> *of happy events. They do not consist in learning to say positive things to yourself.... What is crucial is what you think when you fail, using the power of "non-negative thinking." Changing the destructive things you say to yourself when you experience the setbacks that life deals all of us is the central skill of optimism.*

Changing the way you think about a situation is called *reframing*. It is reframing when you change your conceptual or emotional viewpoint regarding a situation by seeing it in a more positive light, by looking for the silver lining, or by simply maintaining your faith, and that is a key skill in becoming more optimistic.

Seligman found that one's habitual ways of exploring bad and good events are learned from childhood and come from one's personal view of how you fit into the world. He categorized these methods of thinking into the three dimensions: *permanence, pervasiveness,* and *personalization.*

Permanence. This explores how long you feel the consequences of good or bad events will last. For example, very optimistic people view good events as having permanent causes. When these good events occur, optimists will often try even harder in the future. Pessimists often view these events or successes as simply a fluke and still give up.

Pervasiveness. This looks at the extent to which good and bad events impact other areas of your life. Some pessimists experience a catastrophe in one area of their life, and those circumstances then impact other, unconnected areas of their lives such as their work, health, or key relationships. An optimist may get upset about this particular event but recognizes that its effects are limited, and they do not allow it to have an impact on other, unrelated areas.

Personalization. This is the extent to which you blame yourself or others when bad events occur in your life, and also whether you internalize or externalize good events that occur.

This is closely related to your self-esteem levels. People who habitually blame themselves for the bad events in their lives have lower self-esteem.

It should be stated, however, that personalization can be overrated in its impact. A much more important element is your view of permanence. If you believe that the bad events that occur in your life have permanent causes, then you are likely to believe that there is nothing you can do to change this and therefore you will not try to do so.[29]

What's the difference in how this looks for a pessimist vs. an optimist?

A pessimist's view of permanence might manifest in how they view their not receiving a work promotion, for example; they will see it as a permanent problem. "I'll never get promoted," they think. "They don't like me. I'll never get that job."

Pessimists, secondly, show pervasiveness in viewing a problem as if it is affecting all aspects of their entire life. "I'm a failure at everything! We will lose our house. I will shame my parents, my spouse will lose respect for me," they say, "...and

29) (n.d.). Retrieved January 22, 2015, from http://www.actnow.ie/files/Learned-Optimism-Book-Summary.pdf.

all because I didn't get the promotion."

And thirdly, in personalization, pessimists take on too much of the blame. As always, we need to take responsibility for our actions, but there are always things that are outside of our control. Pessimists sometimes can't acknowledge that fact and somehow manage to find themselves at fault for everything, no matter how absurd.

The optimist, on the other hand, displays their idea of permanence in the job situation differently; to them, not getting a promotion is temporary—there's a chance to get it next year. Their pervasiveness shows itself in that they don't allow their disappointment to affect their entire life. "It's only a small part of my life; I still have my health and a great family situation," they think. Their personalization manifests itself by their taking responsibility for their actions but realizing that, since they did their part and it failed to bring about a promotion, then something outside of their control determined their not receiving the job.

So, with all that said, *can* optimism be learned? Some people think that you are born an optimist or a pessimist and you can't change it. But Seligman says no, a pessimist can learn to be an optimist by breaking down these three components and looking at them as you confront different situations. Seeing that things aren't permanent or pervasive and not taking everything as a personal failure are the characteristics of an optimist…and you can train yourself to think that way, and continue to stick with it. When facing a crisis, don't make it more permanent than it is, more pervasive than it is, or more personal than it is. That, essentially, is optimism.

The research is clear: optimists do better in disasters. They suffer less of the negative aspects of stress. In my twenty-five years of policing, I have seen many optimists and pessimists under stress and facing significant obstacles. The optimists still prepare for danger; they just know that despite the gravity of the challenge they are facing, in the end they will triumph over it. Despite the fact they are dealing with the worst society has to offer, they know that people are basically good, that challenges are temporary, and that they can have a positive influence on the outcome. That is why optimism is a key resiliency factor being taught to the U.S. military in the Comprehensive Soldier Fitness Program. It can be learned, it can be used even in demanding combat situations, and it will reduce stress injuries.

My challenge to you: The next time you are facing a difficult situation, reframe it in a more positive light, know that it won't last forever, and have faith that you will prevail!

CHAPTER ELEVEN
RESILIENCY FACTOR:
FINDING MEANING IN SUFFERING

"Out of suffering have emerged the strongest souls; the most massive characters are seared with scars."
Kahlil Gibran

There is power in finding meaning in suffering. According to Victor Frankl, "Everything can be taken from a man but one thing: the last of human freedoms—to choose one's attitude in any given set of circumstances, to choose one's own way."

I've endured several trials in my life, and finding meaning in suffering helped me to not just get back to normalcy, but to grow and create a better quality of life. Like everyone, I've experienced everyday stress, sometimes working in a toxic environment, being overwhelmed with too much stuff on my plate, dealing with complex and difficult demands, and then, of course, the more serious negative events and trauma. Searching for meaning in these stressful times helps build resilience. For example, one very stressful incident happened over twenty years ago, early in my career.

I broke up with my fiancée a few weeks before we were to be married. She was a case preparation clerk for the Internal Affairs Unit, so I shouldn't have been surprised by what happened next—she knew how to get revenge.

She made false allegations against me, saying that I was abusive and racist. I ended up getting arrested and spent the night in jail at my own police station, criminally charged with domestic assault. Even the cops on my shift called me "the prisoner" when they came to visit me in the cell (it was their attempt to bring humor to the situation, and reluctantly I had to admit it was rather funny).

I spent the next year going through the court system to get cleared. Eventually I was exonerated, but it was a long and arduous year filled with stress. I thought I could lose my job, and my career. It was even all over the news. I lost weight, couldn't sleep, and went through a lot of negative reactions to the stress.

Being a police officer, I am exposed to trauma on the job on a regular basis. I've even been robbed and beaten unconscious by a gang in Toronto. Yet that stress wasn't as bad. Getting arrested because of false accusations was much more stressful than getting beaten and robbed. I suffered tremendously for something I did not do. Only my greater sense of purpose kept me afloat during this turbulent time in my life. I believed tests and tribulations happen for a reason, and I knew I would gain something from it, even though I didn't know exactly what at that time.

Having a victim's mentality and allowing yourself to be buffeted around in every direction only prolongs your suffering. I came to see that my responses would make a difference in my outcome. I had to stop the pity party and feeling sorry for myself. Over time, I was able to see the strength I gained by going through a stressful event like this. I found my own personal meaning. I experienced growth. I can look back and appreciate those benefits in a different way now. That also gives me strength going forward, because whatever the severity of the event, I know over time I will find meaning in the experience and become a better person in some way.

Stress is abolished, fear is extinguished, and anxiety is annihilated when you know that there is deep meaning and purpose to your adversity.

EXAMPLES OF OTHERS BEFORE US

Paul was an apostle/evangelist who spread the message of Christianity to Asia and Europe in the years 39 to 68 AD. He experienced a horrendous amount of suffering in his lifetime, yet he wrote thirteen books of the New Testament. In one of his books, he recounted some of his trials:

> *Five times I received from the Jews the forty lashes minus one. Three times I was beaten with rods, once I was pelted with stones, three times I was shipwrecked, I spent a night and a day in the open sea, I have been constantly on the move. I have been in danger from rivers, in danger from bandits, in danger from my fellow Jews, in danger from Gentiles; in danger in the city, in danger in the country, in danger at sea; and in danger from*

false believers. I have labored and toiled and have often gone without sleep; I have known hunger and thirst and have often gone without food; I have been cold and naked. Besides everything else, I face daily the pressure of my concern for all the churches. (2 Corinthians 11:24–28, NIV)

There were many instances, as evidenced by the scripture mentioned above, where Paul's death seemed imminent. What made him resilient was his faith, and the clear meaning he had for his life. He had a mission to fulfill. From the scriptural account and from Paul's writings, we know that he didn't fall apart with what we would consider now as symptoms of PTSD. He was driven by a sense of purpose and by the level of meaning he attached to the work he was doing.

Once you are connected to your purpose in life, the trials and tribulations become easier. This purpose kept Victor Frankl going as he suffered for years in the Nazi concentration camps. (If you have not read Frankl's book, *Man's Search for Meaning*, do yourself a favor and read it.) Even while going through the immense suffering of the Holocaust and being imprisoned at Auschwitz and other concentration camps, he found meaning in the suffering. He imagined himself writing the book and teaching at the university in Vienna after the war. He shows his resiliency in this poignant passage from *Man's Search for Meaning*:

We stumbled on in the darkness, over big stones and through large puddles, along the one road leading from the camp. The accompanying guards kept shouting at us and driving us with the butts of their rifles. Anyone with very sore feet supported himself on his neighbor's arm. Hardly a word was spoken; the icy wind did not encourage talk. Hiding his mouth behind his upturned collar, the man marching next to me whispered suddenly: "If our wives could see us now! I do hope they are better off in their camps and don't know what is happening to us."

That brought thoughts of my own wife to mind. And as we stumbled on for miles, slipping on icy spots, supporting each other time and again, dragging one another up and onward, nothing was said, but we both knew: each of us was thinking of his wife. Occasionally I looked at the sky, where the stars were fading and the pink light of the morning was beginning to spread behind a dark bank of clouds. But my mind clung to my wife's image, imagining it with an uncanny acuteness. I heard her answering me, saw her smile, her frank and encouraging look. Real or not, her look was then more luminous than the sun which was beginning to rise.

A thought transfixed me: for the first time in my life I saw the truth as it is set into song by so many poets, proclaimed as the final wisdom by so many thinkers. The truth—that love is the ultimate and the highest goal to which Man can

> *aspire. Then I grasped the meaning of the greatest secret that human poetry and human thought and belief have to impart: The salvation of Man is through love and in love. I understood how a man who has nothing left in this world still may know bliss, be it only for a brief moment, in the contemplation of his beloved. In a position of utter desolation, when Man cannot express himself in positive action, when his only achievement may consist in enduring his sufferings in the right way—an honorable way—in such a position Man can, through loving contemplation of the image he carries of his beloved, achieve fulfillment. For the first time in my life I was able to understand the meaning of the words, "The angels are lost in perpetual contemplation of an infinite glory."*

That's not what I would have been thinking. I probably would have had thoughts more along the lines of a scene in Quentin Tarantino's *Inglourious Basterds*, imagining carving a swastika into the forehead of the Nazi guard. But good on Victor for being above that and for being an example of how even in the most inhumane of circumstances, we can choose humanity and meaning.

THE GUSH KATIF EFFECT

Sometimes stress caused by betrayal or even feeling isolated and unsupported can be worse than the stress caused by traumatic events. The reason is that it can shatter our worldview. It can crush our spirits and make it difficult to find meaning.

You may find it surprising that the stress of betrayal can actually be worse than traumatic stress. It seems counterintuitive, but let me explain. What really made me consider this was when I heard the story of Gush Katif, a Jewish town that was located within the Gaza Strip. The town was surrounded by their enemies. They were constantly bombarded with Kassam rockets, and when they drove anywhere they often had rocks thrown at their cars. Palestinian militants would try to infiltrate the town to attack them.

Despite the trauma, the townspeople were amazingly resilient and successful. Possibly because they found meaning in making a stand for Israel, and they felt supported by their country. They even had a sense of control over their destiny, because they had chosen to settle there and to not be controlled or intimidated by terrorism. And they did well. They became a vibrant agricultural community that exported organic produce all over Europe.

During the peace process when Israel handed over control of Gaza to the Palestinians in 2005, the Israeli government forced the evacuation of the town of Gush Katif. Many residents did not willingly leave and were forcibly evicted, and their homes were demolished. The Israeli government housed them for years in temporary prefabricated homes in Jewish communities outside of Gaza. After the evacuation, the townspeople were no longer subject to rocket attacks and constant trauma. Surprisingly, the people became less resilient generally. They have more stress-related sickness, more heart disease, more unemployment, and more trouble with their youth. Why? No more rockets. They are safe now! It doesn't seem to make sense, but when I looked deeper into their feelings about what it meant, I began to understand. They felt betrayed by their own government. In their minds they were risking their lives in making a stand for the people of Israel, and then Israel turns around and forces them out of their homes. It took away their meaning.

It made me think of a colleague of mine who, because of his investigative specialty, had been exposed to trauma throughout his policing career. He was able to handle that vicarious trauma on a daily basis without a problem. He found meaning in his expertise and took pride in his work.

Then an incident happened where he felt he had been treated harshly by management. He perceived that he was being persecuted by those above him. That was the beginning of the end of his career. It led to stress leave, health problems, and eventually early retirement. After all the traumatic stress he had endured in his career, it was the organizational stress that finished him. I believe it was because his career had lost its meaning.

Why is betrayal or abandonment particularly distressing? Because it can destroy the purpose we have in our life.

In order to grow from difficulties and trauma, we have to be able to search for and find meaning. Trauma itself is meaningless. It's the meaning that we affix to it that impacts our emotional state. Whatever meaning we choose to attach to our adversity will determine our level of suffering or peace.

CHAPTER TWELVE
RESILIENCY FACTOR: SPIRITUALITY

"We are not human beings having a spiritual experience.
We are spiritual beings having a human experience."
Pierre Teilhard de Chardin, French philosopher

There are not many times that the scientific commu-nity agrees with the religious community, but the case of resiliency is one of those times. The 2005 *Annual Review of Clinical Psychology* said that "religion and spirituality provide a framework for understanding adversity and making sense of tragedy." Research has shown that people who have spiritual beliefs do better in trauma than people who don't have any guiding belief system. It doesn't have to be traditional religious beliefs, but faith in a higher power of some sort has a positive impact on people's ability to cope with traumatic events.

In my own life, there are certain factors that are innate and have been a part of my personality my whole life: I've always been an optimistic person. I've always believed in God and in life after death, and have always been able to step back and look at that eternal perspective. I've had a good support system of family and friends. These resiliency factors I've had in my life all along.

But my faith had a large part to do with my pursuit of a better life. I realized in my early twenties "as [a man] thinketh in his heart, so is he" (Proverbs 23:7). I recognized that the heart, mind, and soul are connected; if one was not well it would make it impossible to live a fulfilled life. That's why I set out to implement other resiliency factors into my life. I wanted to do more than just survive the trials and tribulations in life; I wanted to thrive despite them, and I wanted to grow because of them.

Spirituality can help people find real meaning in life, especially in the difficult times and times of loss. Being spiritually fit can impact your resilience and overall well-being by buffering stress. The reason? As I mentioned in the previous chapter, your personal beliefs about what an incident means will determine to a large extent the amount of distress that you have. If you believe in God, or something bigger than yourself, you will be more likely to find a higher meaning. More likely to look at the eternal perspective.

Spirituality is not a crutch or a sign of weakness. History accurately records many war heroes who were exemplary people of faith.

One of the greatest examples of faith's role in resiliency is the faith of one of the most courageous generals of the Civil

War, Thomas "Stonewall" Jackson. After a severe battle where Jackson was sitting on his horse calmly with bullets flying all around him, a captain asked him, "General, how is it that you can keep so serene with a storm of bullets raining about your head?" Jackson said,

> "My religious belief teaches me to feel as safe in battle as in bed. God has fixed a time for my death, and I do not concern myself with that, but to be always ready whenever it may overtake me. That's the way all men should live; then all men would be equally brave."

It was his religious beliefs that gave him that courage.

This resiliency factor empowers you to look at the bigger picture and view your situation from a transcendent perspective. Dr. Frederic Flach, author of *Resilience: Discovering a New Strength at Times of Stress*, wrote, "I believe the most vital ingredient of resilience is faith. For some, faith will exist within the framework of formal religion. For others it lies within the deepest level of our unconscious minds in touch with eternal truths."[30]

YOUR PERSONAL WALK

The human condition is such that we all must unavoidably experience loss and pain. All of us suffer to a greater or lesser extent, depending on our own personal interpretation of the

---

30) Flach, F. (1988). Resilience: Discovering a new strength at times of stress. New York: Fawcett Columbine.

loss. Your belief about what an incident means and how it fits into the framework of your life will be the measure of the amount of distress you have. And if you believe in something greater than yourself, a higher power, or a purpose in life, you will be more resilient than someone who does not.

Do you believe that everything happens for a reason? The reason for your stress or current difficulty may be that you needed this challenge to grow or that you are being led on a certain path. It doesn't matter what the reason is; just the fact that you have faith in this principle is enough to reduce your stress. I believe this, and can see how it has assisted me when things have gone sideways in my life.

Here's a visualization exercise that you can try. Imagine yourself, eighty years old and near the end of your life. Looking back, see the losses and trials that you have experienced, tempered by time and with the benefit of added wisdom. See how they took your life in a particular direction, how new opportunities opened up or new relationships were forged. In most cases the most meaningful experiences in life were not the easy times, but the times where you faced and overcame adversity.

Don't wait until you're on your deathbed to figure that out. Have faith that all your negative experiences will prepare you for your ultimate purpose.

CHAPTER THIRTEEN

RESILIENCY FACTOR: SELF-CONFIDENCE, SELF-ESTEEM & SELF-EFFICACY

"Because one believes in oneself, one doesn't try
to convince others. Because one is content with oneself,
one doesn't need others' approval. Because one accepts
oneself, the whole world accepts him or her."
Lao Tzu, author of the Tao Te Ching

SELF-CONFIDENCE

Self-confidence is critical in building your capacity to resist stress. If you believe that you can, and are willing to put effort behind your belief, you are able to overcome obstacles and are bound for success. Self-confidence also equips you to put measures in place to help you avoid mental, physical, and spiritual potholes. It can be defined as "the belief that you can achieve success and competence. In other words—believing yourself to be capable. Self-confidence might be in reference to specific tasks or a more wide-ranging attitude you hold about your abilities in life."[31]

Dr. Clemens Kirschbaum did a study where he tested a group of people for cortisol levels before they gave a public address. The participants were required to do a speech in front of people every day of the study. The result was that over time 95 percent of the participants had less cortisol and less stress by the fifth public address. The 5 percent that had the same amount of stress and did not adapt were the participants who had low self-confidence. Low self-confidence is a dream killer.

So how do you overcome a dream killer? Well, let's see how Amy Cuddy did it.

In *Your Body Language Shapes Who You Are*, social psychologist Amy Cuddy describes one of the biggest traumas she ever had to face in life. Cuddy describes how as a young adolescent her intelligence was her pride and joy. Unfortunately, when she was nineteen years old, she was in a serious car accident and was thrown out of a car. She woke up with a head injury that was so severe that her I.Q. dropped by two standard deviations. The essence of who she was, her intellectual capital, was lost.

She ended up leaving college, heartbroken. She tried several times to go back but was faced with resistance because of her disability. She was persistent, though, and kept trying, eventually graduating from college even though it took her four years longer than the average student to do it. But she did it.

When she was a grad student at Princeton, she suffered from impostor syndrome, feeling like she wasn't supposed to be there. Cuddy said that she often felt like a fraud. That feeling

---

31) Developing Self Confidence, Self Esteem and Resilience. (2009, January 1). Retrieved January 22, 2015, from http://mams.rmit.edu.au/elh5d4nc7sfd.pdf.

took its toll on her the night before she was to give her first-year twenty-minute talk to twenty people. She called her advisor the next day and quit.

Her doctoral advisor, Susan Fiske, told Amy that she was not quitting because Fiske had taken a gamble on her. Cuddy was staying. Fiske told her to act as if she had confidence, to "fake it."

Later, when Cuddy was teaching at Harvard and one of her students said to her, "I'm not supposed to be here," that she felt like a fraud, Cuddy had her "Ah-ha" moment. She realized that she herself didn't feel that way anymore. She had "faked it" until she *became* it, like her advisor had said. Cuddy had really learned self-confidence by pretending to have it until it was real.

After you fake it for a while, your mind and how you think about yourself changes, and so does your level of confidence. Cuddy's point is not simply "Fake it 'til you make it," but "Fake it 'til you *become* it." [32]

She has since done more research into confidence at Harvard. What she has found is that a good way to become more confident is through controlling your body language. Expand your body, open up, "get big," take up space. Cuddy's research shows that our nonverbal behavior governs not only how other people think about us, but also how we think and feel about ourselves. If we act powerful and confident, we will start to feel powerful and confident.

This is because it actually has an impact on our hormones, too. High-power and confident people have more testosterone

---

32) Cuddy, A. Phd (2012, June 1). Your body language shapes who you are. TEDGlobal 2012. Lecture conducted from Edinburgh, Scotland.

(dominance hormone) and less cortisol (stress hormone). Low-power people with less self-confidence have less testosterone and more cortisol. The cool part of Cuddy's research was the discovery that if you fake being confident with your body language, it actually changes your bio-chemicals. When you fake confidence, your testosterone goes up and your cortisol goes down. By acting confident, you become confident and your stress hormones are reduced, and you feel stronger, more powerful, and more resilient.

SELF-ESTEEM

The experts say that,

> *Self-esteem is defined as your opinion of yourself and your worth. In other words, your perception of your value as a person, particularly with regard to the work you do, your status, achievements, purpose in life, your perceived place in the social order, potential for success, strengths and weaknesses, how you relate to others, and your ability to stand on your own feet.*[33]

The exact opposite is when you devalue your self-worth and hold yourself in low esteem. Low self-esteem can result in the following health challenges:

- Negative thinking patterns associated with low self-

---

33) Developing Self Confidence, Self Esteem and Resilience. (2009, January 1). Retrieved January 22, 2015, from http://mams.rmit.edu.au/elh5d4nc7sfd.pdf.

esteem can develop over time and lead to mental health problems such as depression or anxiety.

- The negative emotions associated with low self-esteem can weaken your immune system.

- Low self-esteem can make it hard to try new things or complete tasks, particularly when it omes to building resiliency.

- Feelings of low self-esteem and lack of control can increase your risk of heart disease and high blood pressure.

Over the past century, we have heard experts say that having a strong belief in self is more than half of the battle. In one article, Nan Henderson, M.S.W. says,

> *I believe what people of all ages need is the "resiliency route to authentic self-esteem and life success." This type of self-esteem is not the mere fluff of meaningless affirmations. It is based on recognizing actual accomplishment, identifying and understanding how we have and can use our strengths, and living a life filled with expressions of our unique "talents and gifts."*[34]

Keep in mind that we have an innate capacity to bounce

34) Henderson M.S.W., N. (n.d.). The Resiliency Route to Authentic Self-Esteem and Life Success. Retrieved January 22, 2015, from https://www.resiliency.com/free-articles-resources/the-resiliency-route-to-authentic-self-esteem-and-life-success/.

back. We all have it, but some may not be aware of it. I suggest that you deliberately sit down and identify what your strengths are. Interview yourself and make a list of your gifts, talents, skills, etc. Then compare them to the resiliency factors listed in this book. This will help you identify your strengths so that you can readily use them when the occasion requires, and also help you determine the areas that you may need to build up. Doing so will allow you to see patterns in your life, and see your successes. Rehearsing past victories is a good way to support your innate capacity for resilience and build up your self-esteem. Do this often, and you will soon find your self-esteem growing.

SELF-EFFICACY

Self-efficacy is different from self-confidence in that it is more objective, whereas self-confidence is more subjective. Self-confidence is more of a feeling based on your emotions, which can go up or down based on what is happening during your day. Self-efficacy is your analytical judgment about the specific skills that you have in order to deal with a specific stressor. More skills equals more self-efficacy, which equals less stress. In other words:

> *Perceived self-efficacy is defined as people's beliefs about their capabilities to produce designated levels of performance that exercise influence over events that affect their lives. Self-efficacy beliefs determine how people feel, think, motivate*

themselves, and behave.[35]

Self-efficacy removes the uncertainty that a traumatic situation can have a positive ending. Resiliency is often robust because of the individual's preparation prior to the event.

Several years ago I was on a search halfway between Cochrane and Moosonee. It's in Northern Ontario, a remote area about a hundred miles from the nearest road. It was winter, and snowing, and about minus ten degrees Fahrenheit. Three of us were dropped off by helicopter. The pilot told us that if the weather got any worse he wouldn't be back for three days, which was when it was supposed to clear. We had no communications with the outside world either, because this was in the days before satellite phones. We had all done winter survival training, and because of that we had trust in our abilities and skill with our equipment, and therefore we each had a high level of self-efficacy. There was no stress because we perceived the demand as low. Someone else in the same situation may have a lot of distress, because of fear, or not knowing if they could survive. It would be a high demand. But because of our judgment of our capacity to handle adverse weather and survival needs, it was not stressful at all. We knew we could handle whatever happened in this situation. It was a judgment of our level of self-efficacy.

As you increase your skills you will become more confident and resilient. And there's no shame in admitting that you aren't where you need to be; the truth is you can't get better until you know where you are now. So analyze your confidence, esteem,

35) Bandura, A. (1994). Self-efficacy. In V. S. Ramachaudran (Ed.), Encyclopedia of human behavior (Vol. 4, pp. 71-81). New York: Academic Press. (Reprinted in H. Friedman [Ed.], Encyclopedia of mental health. San Diego: Academic Press, 1998.)

and efficacy, and then begin working on each of them until you reach a high level. Remember, it doesn't hurt to "fake it" until you *become* it!

CHAPTER FOURTEEN
RESILIENCY FACTOR:
FEEL IN CONTROL

"Incredible change happens in your life when you
decide to take control of what you do have power over
instead of craving control over what you don't."
Steve Maraboli, author

It is part of the human condition to want to be in absolute
control of the events in our lives. We can't accomplish such
a lofty deed in an unpredictable world…but we do have *some*
measure of control over our lives.

Realizing that is what keeps you healthy and resilient. If you
feel as though you don't have any control, then it's a downhill
slide, possibly into passivity or depression. You become
susceptible to the will of anyone and anything, opening the
door to defeat and despair when a crisis appears.

Martin Seligman developed a theory called "learned
helplessness." It is defined as a state of mind where "people feel

helpless to avoid negative situations because previous experience has shown them that they do not have control."[36] In 1985, Seligman started doing research on classical conditioning, which is the process where a human or animal associates one thing with another, usually referred to in conjunction with Pavlov's work. Seligman, in his research, would ring a bell and shock a dog at the same time. Eventually the dog would only have to hear the bell ring to respond as if it had been traumatized, even though the actual stimulus had not been applied.

Seligman then moved the dog to a crate that was divided by a low fence. The dog could see the other side of the crate and had the ability to jump over if necessary. The floor on one side of the fence was normal; on the other side of the fence the floor was electrified. He put the dog on the electrified side of the fence, as well as several other dogs that hadn't been shocked before. Those dogs would just jump over the fence to the safe side. The first dog, however, remained on the electrified side, just taking the shocks. It had become accustomed to not being able to escape, and felt helpless to avoid the shocks. It had developed a "learned helplessness" that prevented it from being able to do what was necessary to remove itself out of harm's way.

Some people take pride in being victims. They make their identity all about being a victim, complaining, whining, blaming others instead of taking responsibility and changing it. Eckart Tolle said, "Many people continue to suffer because they keep the past alive and then build an identity around it."

36) Boyd, N. (n.d.). How Seligman's Learned Helplessness Theory Applies to Human Depression and Stress.

Do you know any people that are like Seligman's dog? All they have to do to avoid some stressor in their life is hop over a short fence—to take control of the situation—but they refuse to do it.

Harry Mills, Ph.D. and Mark Dombeck, in their article "Resilience: Control" identified control as both primary control and secondary. "Primary control," as they define it, "involves the ability to actually change a situation. Secondary control involves the ability to change how you think about a situation."[37] A good example of having primary control over a situation is when someone is in an abusive situation. It may not be easy for them to leave, but they must if they are to improve their self-esteem and the overall quality of their lives. Secondary control comes into play when an unchangeable life event like a death in the family occurs; you realize that there is nothing that you can physically do about it, but you can look at the situation in the most positive light possible.

Even if a situation is out of your control, like most critical incidents, you always have some measure of control *of yourself* and how you *think* about the situation. There is always something you can do, even if it's just planning your own survival. The first step to regaining control is to accept your situation, whatever it is. Then you must act on even the smallest aspect you can. The less control you have, the more distress you will feel, true—but there is always something you can do to feel in control. It's about how much control you *think* you have. Once you exercise the control you believe you

37) Mental Health, Depression, Anxiety, Wellness, Family & Relationship Issues, Sexual Disorders & ADHD Medications. (n.d.). Retrieved January 24, 2015, from http://www.mentalhelp.net/poc/view_doc.php?type=doc&id=5792.

have, you will find yourself feeling less distress.

For example, take a look at students in a cafeteria during an active shooter incident. Some will freeze and wait to die; others, on the other hand, will use tables to create cover, or try to escape. Research suggests that those that take some action will be less inclined to get PTSD than those that do nothing. But the more surprising part is, even if the student doesn't get to put their plan into action, even if it's just planning what they are going to do, they will be less inclined to get PTSD. It's because they feel more powerful, more in control, as opposed to feeling helpless.

The same goes for you. Realizing that you have some control over how you respond to any situation will increase your resiliency.

EXPECTANCY

Unlike some people who just let life "happen" to them, you can learn to expect adversity and problems in life. If you know bad things are going to happen at some point, then it won't come as a total shock. Attitude and preparation is the key to not being overwhelmed.

I knew at an early age that I wanted to be in law enforcement. I grew up in the eighties, and was influenced by shows like *Miami Vice* and *Magnum, P.I.* (my two favorite shows) and other action-packed movies that reinforced my desire to live a life with lots of action. So when I became an adult and pursued my career, I felt ready for the stressors that are associated with the trauma of policing.

Some people have a totally different reason for going into law enforcement. They may be pursuing that career for job security or because it has a secure pension and a good health plan. When it comes to dealing with the traumatic events that are associated with the job, these people's expectations may be influenced by those things rather than their passion for action and adventure.

Let me demonstrate with an example. Consider two cops racing to a shooting in progress. As they are driving there at high speeds, one is feeling excited; the first one became a cop because of the desire for action. (Maybe the *Miami Vice* theme song is even playing in their head. Really—it happens!) The other one, meanwhile, is feeling uptight. They became a cop because it was a secure job during the economic downturn. As they are both going to this dangerous call, who is feeling more stress? It will be the one who is thinking, *Man, I didn't sign up for this.*

As mentioned earlier, accepting the situation you are in—or are going into—is a key factor in resilience. You need to understand where you are at and then mentally prep yourself for the likely stressors you will face. You should *expect* them and be ready for them. Then you will feel more in control.

As you may have figured out by this point in the book, all resiliency factors can be developed and learned. That includes expectancy. Here are some tips for developing a healthy expectancy.

- Be realistic in your expectations. What are the stressors related to your career? Mentally prepare for those stressors. Visualize yourself going through that specific challenge successfully.

- Create your expectancy around your desired performance, building it on your past performances (your successes), your self-confidence (your strengths), and the perceived difficulty of your goal (your reality).

- Keep your "why" close to you. For example: I am going to physical therapy, regardless of the pain I experience, because I expect to walk again.

- Attribute a value to the reward that you are seeking that will keep you focused on the intrinsic or extrinsic compensation that you expect to receive. In my case, my reward in writing this book is that it will help others become more resilient so that they can avoid some of the pain and stress that are common in the modern workplace.

Being in control of your thoughts and having the expectation that bad things will happen, but also having the positive expectation that everything is going to eventually work out for your good, can contribute to your ability to bounce back. Being honest with yourself about the reality of your situation and finding the aspects of it that you can control will help you grow from trauma instead of being injured by it.

If you prepare your mind for those inevitable traumas in life, when they show up you'll be more ready for them and resiliency will be second nature to you.

Just before I actually started in law enforcement, I had

the unfortunate experience of getting robbed and beaten to the point of unconsciousness by five gangbangers. I experienced numerous injuries and a concussion, but my perspective was that sometimes you lose a fight. No big deal. I had seen my heroes—like Magnum, P.I.—lose fights and I figured it was part of the job that I wanted to do. If my expectancy had been slightly different, if I had expected to never get in a fight in my life, my outcome could have possibly been a stress injury or PTSD. If I had a victim mentality and felt no control, maybe I would have developed PTSD. But I had some feeling of control. I fought back. I didn't give up until I was unconscious. I thought maybe if it was only two instead of five I could have won. I had trained in martial arts so I had self-confidence in my ability to defend myself, but I was also realistic in that I didn't expect to be able to defend myself against five people.

Earlier we talked about feeling in control. In this instance I was in control of my attitude about what happened and the way I handled myself during the fight. I also had the expect-ancy that I was going to get into fights and some I would win and some I would lose. It wasn't a permanent defeat but a temporary learning experience. And I didn't feel any stress reaction because of it. I just gained a cool "war story" to share with my friends. Not a bad outcome.

Ryan Holiday, a follower of stoic philosophy, in his book *The Obstacle Is the Way: The Timeless Art of Turning Adversity to Advantage*, says, "The only guarantee, ever, is that things will go wrong. The only thing we can use to mitigate this is anticipation. Because the only variable we control completely is ourselves."

I've heard stories of paramedics who have been diagnosed with PTSD because they watched a person die. They publically complain about the incident and their organization, feeling like a victim and placing blame everywhere else. But really, what did they expect was going to happen as a paramedic? CPR is only 10% effective outside of hospitals, meaning 90% of people who CPR is performed on… *die*! They know going into it that they're going to lose a lot of people, *or they should know*. What have they done to prepare for that certain eventuality and what have they done after the trauma to treat the stress?

If you are going into a career in emergency services, you can expect that you will be in danger and that you will see dead people. The employers have a duty to train you and a duty to help you mentally prepare for the trauma that you will be exposed to, but you also have a duty to yourself. You know what to expect. What are you doing to prepare yourself? This goes back to Seligman's dogs and learned helplessness. If you know what to expect and are prepared, then you will feel in control. Take some action to help yourself.

This is true for all careers, not just emergency services. High school teachers have a different set of stressors than Wall Street traders. Palliative care nurses have different stressors than Silicon Valley coders. But the specific stressors commonly related to each career can be anticipated and prepared for. If you expect trouble, mentally prepare for it, and feel in control, then you will be more successful in your career. Don't be a victim, be a victor!

CHAPTER FIFTEEN

RESILIENCY FACTOR: STRESS INOCULATION

> "You have to risk going too far to
> discover just how far you can go."
> *T.S. Eliot*

In ancient Greece, the Spartans dedicated their lives to hardcore battle training. Their training was so intense, for them battle was a reprieve. Spartan children were placed in military-style education programs and trained throughout their youth. All men were expected to be lifelong soldiers. This is not an endorsement of that lifestyle; however, it illustrates why they were the toughest nation of the time. For a Spartan, surrender in battle was the ultimate disgrace.[38]

Their greatest glory came from being a good warrior and emerging from a well-fought battle victorious. They trained hard so that they could build a capacity for physical and mental toughness on the battlefield.

---

38) 8 Reasons It Wasn't Easy Being Spartan. (2013, March 5). Retrieved January 23, 2015, from http://www.history.com/news/history-lists/8-reasons-it-wasnt-easy-being-spartan.

When a person is inoculated against a virus, they build up resistance to that virus and the sickness that it causes. When a person is inoculated against stress, they build up resistance to that stressor and the negative impact it has on emotional well-being.

Stress inoculation is similar to a regular inoculation in several ways. For an inoculation against disease to be effective, it must...

1. **Be Specific.** You have to target the specific virus. A smallpox vaccine won't inoculate you against mumps. You have to have a specific vaccine for each virus that you want to inoculate for. Each year the new flu vaccine contains inoculation against various strains of the flu that they anticipate will be circulating. If they pick the wrong strains, then the vaccine is ineffective.

2. **Be Realistic.** They use the real virus in a weakened form.

3. **Allow Victory.** Too much will overwhelm the system and make you sick. If the virus was too strong, it would just cause the disease, as opposed to teaching your system to overcome it. Your body must be able to win.

If an inoculation follows these steps, then, when you are exposed to the virus, it doesn't make you sick. You have built up resistance, or immunity, to that *bug*.

Stress Inoculation is the same. Exposing yourself to stress

in a training environment inoculates you against stress. Then, when you have real-world stress, you have built up immunity, or resistance to that stressor. You don't get sick, or suffer from adverse effects.

Like with regular inoculation, stress inoculation has to:

1. **Be Specific.** You have to train for each specific stressor independently. One type of training does not inoculate you against all types of stress.

2. **Be Realistic.** You have to make the training as realistic as possible.

3. **Allow Victory.** You can't overwhelm the person with stress in the training, or they won't grow and build resistance to that stressor.

That third point is critical. Lt. Col. David Grossman (Retired) says it's critical that the person emerge victorious from the training, so they know they can handle the real event, and so they won't give up when the chips are down. The person doesn't have to win the scenario every time, they can lose some scenarios, but by the end of the training they need to win. If the person doesn't win in the stress inoculation training, it can be like Seligman's dogs with learned helplessness (which we covered in the previous chapter, *Feel in Control*). The person will just give up when faced with that stress. They will have a victim mentality and not take action to fight, because they believe they can't win.

So the key is inducing the correct amount of stress. Not enough, and they won't grow, won't achieve immunity. Too much, and they will be overwhelmed and it will be more than their system can handle. Like giving someone a healthy virus in a vaccine, they would just get the disease. So it's like exercise: you have to hit the target heart rate, but not go over the maximum heart rate, to get the optimal health benefit. With this, you have to understand the upper limit of stress. Make sure they are being stressed, but not overwhelmed, and make sure they win in the end. Then they will achieve the greatest benefit, and will have increased immunity to that stressor.

Sometimes we inoculate ourselves against certain stressors without doing formal training. Through our normal work or life experience as we deal with certain stress on a regular basis, we get used to it and build up immunity to that type of stress. Author Jim Loehr, in his book *Toughness Training for Life*, says, *"Stress that toughens falls between maintenance stress and excessive stress...distinguishing between insufficient stress and maintenance stress and also between adaptive stress and excessive stress—it's a vital toughening skill."*[39]

Following are some examples of stress inoculation training and how it works:

FIREFIGHTERS:

They have to train with real fire. They can't train with fake flames, like pieces of orange plastic blowing with a fan to look like flames. It has to be real fire. They have to feel the heat.

---

39) Loehr, J. (1993). *Toughness training for life: A revolutionary program for maximizing health, happiness, and productivity.* New York: Dutton.

1. It is specific training to what they do. That kind of training won't inoculate them against relationship stress. But it will work for the stress of fighting a house fire.

2. It is realistic training. Real cars burning, or real flames in a live fire building.

3. And they can't get seriously injured in the training. They have to win. Otherwise, they would never run into a burning house to rescue a person. They would feel too much stress and fear.

POLICE:

For Immediate Rapid Deployment (IRD):

Before Columbine, police were trained to isolate and contain a gunman and call the SWAT team. At Columbine, while officers were waiting outside the school, containing it, waiting for SWAT, there were kids inside being killed. Police forces across North America realized they had to change their tactics and training.

But this would be a change in mindset for front-line officers. Instead of waiting for the tactical team with the heavy equipment, sniper rifles, etc., they would have to run in and run towards the sound of the shots, something that would cause a high level of stress if not trained properly.

So police forces started doing a lot of IRD training, which turned out to be effective stress inoculation training.

1. It was specific to school shooter situations. We would

actually do training in schools on Saturday when kids weren't there, or in older schools that had been closed.

2. It was realistic. We used screaming and gunshot soundtracks to sound like a real situation. We had role players running through the halls and injured lying in the halls with fake wounds. We used real guns that had Simunition or other marking cartridges, like paintballs. The role players playing the bad guys had the same thing, so if we got shot, it hurt and we knew we were shot.

3. Obviously, we had to win. Not every time, because it's important to push us, to train hard, to stretch us. But in the end we had to win, in the end we had to emerge victorious. If not, if we die every time...no cop would ever want to run into the school. The resistance or immunity comes because it doesn't overwhelm us. We beat it. So we build that resistance.

I'm a Public Order Unit Commander, and before that I was a squad leader and regular member of the Public Order Unit (POU)—or riot cops, as some people know us.

Fifteen years ago the training wasn't as good as it is now. We did not have live fire training with Molotov cocktails. Back then we didn't have the proper equipment, either; we did not have Nomex fire-retardant coveralls to go over the pads. The first time we went to training where we had the new equipment and were being trained with firebombs, a leader asked us, "Do you consider a person throwing a Molotov cocktail as a danger capable of causing serious bodily harm or death?" Many people put up their hands and said, "Yes." That means they would be willing to shoot and kill a protester throwing a Molotov cocktail, because police are trained to shoot when the danger is capable of causing serious bodily harm or death.

But then we did the training, and we learned the capability of our equipment, and we practiced the tactics, such as how to hold our shields and helmets to direct the flames and fumes away from our faces. We walked through the flames without injury, and we realized it wasn't that bad. With the proper equipment and training, a Molotov cocktail would not harm us.

So after the training, the leader asked the same question: "Is a Molotov cocktail capable of causing serious bodily harm or death?" And the answer from everyone was "No." Not when it's a Public Order Unit with the proper equipment and training.

Officers going through that training would feel much less stress in an actual riot, with Molotov cocktails being thrown, than they would have felt before that realistic training. So the stress inoculation training reduces stress, but it also increases performance and decision-making in high-stress situations.

After that training it is much less likely that a protester throwing a firebomb would be shot and killed by police. They may be shot with an anti-riot weapon with rubber bullets or tear gas, instead of a gun, which would reduce the further stress of negative media attention, excessive force investigations, potential charges, lawsuits, etc.

I have seen officers very relaxed in protests where we were outnumbered and people were throwing rocks and bottles at us. We would actually enjoy it, feel the fun and excitement of the event. That's because the operational event is less violent than our training. So it's not a big deal. Officers have less fear, less stress, less anxiety, because they've been there and done that in training.

The Spartans' training was so violent and brutal that they were happy to go to war. Only in battle did they get a reprieve from the hard training that built their resistance.

Like they say in the military, "The more you sweat in training, the less you bleed in battle."

HOW DOES THIS APPLY TO PEOPLE WHO WORK A CORPORATE JOB?

Figure out what aspect of the job stresses you and design a customized stress inoculation training. For example, if you are stressed about difficult conversations, do a training scenario before the actual conversation. Role play with a coworker. Make it specific, realistic, and resulting in success in the end. You will do better and be less stressed in the actual event. You can design stress inoculation for a number of different types of work stress.

It can even be a mental rehearsal. It's better if it engages all your senses and body, but even doing mental rehearsal and visualizing yourself going through it and being victorious will lower the stress when you actually do it.

I have personally used this now that I am in management, with difficult conversations, such as when someone is being disciplined or fired. I role play the situation with one of my administration staff members ahead of time so I'm more mentally and emotionally prepared for what may take place.

Thompson and McCreary cited these as the "Effects of Stress Inoculation Training":

1. Increased ability to cope with stress.

2. Improved performance in high-stress situations.

3. Improved ability to control behavior and response.

Our highest aim is to be prepared for life's catastrophes. The US Army Combat Stress Control Handbook says, "*To achieve greater tolerance or acclimatization to a physical stressor, a progressively greater exposure is required. The exposure should be sufficient to produce more than the routine stress reflexes.*"[40] The Spartans had the right idea.

What are the biggest stressors in your job? Expose yourself to that stress in a controlled training environment and you will build resistance to that stress.

40) Stress Inoculation Training for Coping with Stressors. (n.d.). Retrieved January 23, 2015, from http://www.apa.org/divisions/div12/rev_est/sit_stress.html.

CHAPTER SIXTEEN

RESILIENCY FACTOR: ACCEPTING REALITY

"God, grant me the serenity to accept the things
I cannot change, courage to change the things I can,
and wisdom to know the difference."
The Serenity Prayer

To be effective in stressful and demanding circum-stances, you have to have a realistic assessment of the situation. You can't be in denial and still take effective action. You have to accept your situation. That doesn't mean giving up, or quitting. Accepting reality is sometimes a hard thing to do.

Because of modern technology, we can often have a front row seat to the inconceivable reality of the horrors of our day. This first started happening during the Vietnam War. A little square electronic box made all the difference in the way Americans felt about the war in Vietnam. The power of the pen was superseded by the power of the video.

Today the Internet has taken center stage and knowledge

of worldwide disasters is available for viewing in the midst of the event through the use of smartphone technology. Tonight I took a break from writing and watched the news and saw a young Jordanian pilot burned to death in a cage by the terrorist group ISIS. Yet we also live in a world that gives us much more opportunity to access tools and resources to become stronger when we are faced with the realities of our life's journey. A school kid in central Africa has access to more of the combined world knowledge than President Bill Clinton had at the time of his presidency. It is our choice what we access and how to use it. But we have to accept that in this world there is both humanity and inhumanity, at all times. Acceptance allows you the peace to live through the best and worst times with courage and grace.

Research shows that acceptance of your situation makes you psychologically healthier. In a National survey shortly after the terrorist attacks on the Twin Towers of the World Trade Center, researchers found that those who had accepted the situation had reduced levels of PTSD.[41] Acceptance is a key ingredient in the ability to tolerate highly stressful situations, as demonstrated by survivors of extreme hardship and threats to life.[42]

Some clinical psychologists use a therapy called Acceptance and Commitment Therapy (ACT) which uses *acceptance* as a starting point for taking action to address problems. Research suggests that it is effective in the treatment of stress and anxiety

41) Silver, R.C., Holman, E.A., McIntosh, D.N., Poulin,M., & Gil-Rivas, V. (2002) National longitudinal study of psychological responses to September 11th. Journal of the American Medical Association, 288, 1235-1244.
42) Siebert, A. (1996) The Survivor Personality. New York NY. Pedigree Books.

disorders, as well as other disorders.[43]

The Serenity Prayer made famous by Alcoholics Anonymous should become your mantra when you are in the midst of accepting the reality of a traumatic situation. You must readily accept situations that are not within your control before measuring your capacity to change them. Sometimes the prayer is not to change the situation, but to change yourself so that you can move on. Learning when to let go of control can be as empowering as knowing when to implement it in your life.

Almost 2000 years ago, the Stoic philosopher Epictetus wrote, "What, then, is to be done? To make the best of what is in our power, and take the rest as it naturally happens." You can't allow yourself to become too idealistic, expecting the world to be a perfect place to live, when that will never be the case. No amount of control can guarantee that result. Accepting the reality of your struggle and taking the necessary steps to overcome it is how you become resilient in the midst of tragedy.

Another important aspect of acceptance is accepting ourselves. Often our self-talk is worse than anything we would say to someone else. "If we are to nurture a resilient mindset, we must learn to accept ourselves. Acceptance implies possessing realistic expectations and goals, recognizing our strengths as well as our vulnerabilities, and leading an authentic, balanced life in which our behaviors are in accord with our values and goals. When people are not authentic, they are likely to

43)Southwick, S. & Charney, D. Resilience: The Science of Mastering Life's Greatest Challenges. (2012) Cambridge University Press.

experience increased stress and pressure."[44]

Bruce Lee said, "Be like Water." He was teaching his student to be formless, shapeless, and adaptable. It is also a lesson in resilience.

Every kid likes to throw stones into a pond to watch the splash and the diverging ripples. The circles expand, but then disappear within seconds. It doesn't matter how big the rock is, or the size of the disturbance, the water will quickly regain its form, stability, and calmness.

The pond doesn't ask when hit with a rock, "Why me? Why can't that kid throw a rock into some other pond?" Like water, resilient people have the ability to accept the things they cannot change. With that acceptance comes the calming of the water.

Be like water when hit with the stones that life tosses at you. The concentric circles represent the impact to your soul, mind, or other aspects of life. Like the pond, though, let the impact dissipate quickly. I'll admit that it's easier said than done. All healthy changes are.

Everyone has stress in their lives and the sooner you can let go of it, the happier you will be. A river has great strength and power, but it also has flexibility. It bends where the earth bends. Increasing our acceptance, flexibility, and adaptability will increase our resistance to stress, and our ability to bounce back quickly after trauma.

When I went through my separation, it was hard for me to accept what had happened. I didn't expect it or want it. I'd

---

44) Brooks, R. & Goldstein, S (2004) *The Power of Resilience: Achieving Balance, Confidence, and Personal Strength in Your Life*. McGraw Hill.

ask "why?" and I'd get caught up in rumination and endless thought loops going back in time and not getting anywhere. I'd find myself in a maze of repetitive thoughts and couldn't accept my situation.

I went on a week-long hunting trip to a remote area and was staying in a prospector tent. When I wasn't hunting I was reading *Slaughterhouse Five*. It's a satirical novel by Kurt Vonnegut about the World War II experiences and journeys through time of a soldier named Billy Pilgrim. Billy "becomes unstuck in time" and he experiences moments from various points in his life, past and future. He has no control over when it happens or where he goes. He bounces between being a prisoner of war in Germany during the Dresden fire-bombings, to being held captive in a zoo on the planet of Tralfamadore, to other almost equally unsatisfying times of his life. On Tralfamadore he meets a fellow prisoner, Montana Wildhack, who wears a necklace with a locket, and engraved on the outside of the locket were these words: *"God grant me the serenity to accept the things I cannot change, courage to change the things I can, and wisdom always to tell the difference"*. It was a version of the serenity prayer that I had heard before, but I hadn't thought to really apply it in my life. Throughout the novel the author employs the refrain "So it goes" when death, dying, and other horrendous incidents occur. He does this for comic relief and to explain the unexplained. It reminded me that life isn't fair, so I need to accept my situation. Despite the fantastical nature of the book, it helped me reach a level of acceptance that I hadn't experienced up until then. While reading, I got to the point of not only acceptance on an intellectual level, but also emotionally *feeling* acceptance of my life. So, according to the Serenity Prayer I need to accept the things I cannot change, and according to Vonnegut, "So it goes..."

CHAPTER SEVENTEEN

RESILIENCY FACTOR: FLEXIBILITY

"It is not the strongest or the most intelligent who will survive but those who can best manage change."
Charles Darwin

B e flexible; embrace change. It is inevitable. To be resilient you must be flexible. Resilient people understand that things change, and that carefully-made plans may, occasionally, need to be amended or discarded. Learning how to be adaptable better prepares you for life's ups and downs. Resilient people aren't afraid to venture out in new directions when a road that they were traveling is obliterated.

Diane Coutu wrote in her 2002 HBR article *How Resilience Works,* "Resilient people possess an uncanny ability to improvise." A critical characteristic of resilient people is their capacity to improvise solutions to problems even when they may not have the appropriate resources or proper tools. Resilient individuals make the most of whatever resources are available to them. They imagine possibilities and see connections in situations where less resilient individuals would likely become stymied and discouraged.

Remember the fable about the donkey that was pushed into a hole to die? As his owner was shoveling dirt into the hole to bury him alive, the donkey kept shaking off the dirt and used it as a platform to climb out of the hole to freedom. The moral of this story is, some people may be crushed by adversity but resilient people make the necessary changes to survive. Misfortune will disrupt your life, that's a promise. People who are set in their ways don't do well when faced with hardship. If you're flexible in life you'll do better when adversity comes knocking at your door.

Let's take a look at mental flexibility. According to *www.mentalflexibility.com*, "The essence of mental flexibility is the ability to handle different situations in different ways, especially to respond effectively to new, complex, and problematic situations. The mentally flexible person is able to:

- see things from several different perspectives

- tolerate ambiguity and uncertainty

- take risks willingly

- adapt to change

- learn from mistakes

- solve problems in new ways

- switch between practical and non-practical thinking."[45]

45) What is mental flexibility? (n.d.). Retrieved January 24, 2015, from http://www.mentalflexibility.com/2012/08/26/what-is-mental-flexibility-2/.

All of these strategies are key components of a resilient mind. As mentioned in the last chapter on accepting reality, the world we now live in is very different compared to many years ago. Always remember to "Improvise, Adapt, Overcome." (U.S. Marines' unofficial motto, made famous in the Clint Eastwood movie *Heartbreak Ridge*.)

According to the American Psychological Association, "Resilience involves maintaining flexibility and balance in your life as you deal with stressful circumstances and traumatic events. This happens in several ways, including: Letting yourself experience strong emotions, and also realizing when you may need to avoid experiencing them at times in order to continue functioning. Stepping forward and taking action to deal with your problems and meet the demands of daily living, and also stepping back to rest and re-energize yourself. Spending time with loved ones to gain support and encouragement, and also nurturing yourself. Relying on others, and also relying on yourself."[46]

Like a rubber band that stretches to accommodate its purpose, you will also have to stretch in order to bounce back after adversity. Stretching isn't always easy, but it is necessary. You may have to stretch to chart a new pathway or to reach what you previously perceived to be unreachable, but when you consider the alternative—breaking—being flexible becomes a lot easier.

"The stiffest tree is most easily cracked, while bamboo or willow survives by bending with the

---

46) The Road To Resilience. (n.d.). Retrieved January 24, 2015, from http://www.apa.org/helpcenter/road-resilience. aspx.

wind." – *Bruce Lee*

Dr. Glenn Schiraldi in *The Complete Guide to Resilience* writes, "Peak performers have the ability to adapt to changing situations. They can shift gears when standard procedures aren't working. They make a good plan, but are aware of how the plan is working, and realize when it's not working and can let go of that plan. Effective copers are rooted in self and values, but can bend when bending is called for, as opposed to being rigid at all costs."

In *Deep Survival: Who Lives, Who Dies, and Why* by Laurence Gonzales, the author says, "Don't fall in love with the plan. Be open to a new changing world and let go of the plan when necessary so that you can make a new plan." It reminds me of something that happened to me a few years ago that has become a metaphor for this.

I was in Northern Ontario on a fishing trip, and my friend and I were fishing for smallmouth bass. We had a two-pound bass on the stringer hanging over the side of the boat. Ron got my attention and pointed to the stringer. I noticed a three-foot-long northern pike eyeing up the bass. It then attacked our bass and started shaking it side to side, and scales and meat were being torn off and floating in the water. In my miniaturized version of *The Old Man and The Sea,* my first thought was to get rid of this pike that was ruining my fish. I grabbed the stringer to shake him loose. But as I did that he just hung on. I realized I might be able to catch this pike. I lifted the stringer out of the water, and the pike kept his teeth sunk into the sides of the bass. All he had to do to get away was just open his mouth and drop back into the water. I lifted the stringer over the gunwale of the boat, and put it and the bass and the pike right into the boat. Then the fight with this three-foot-long pike was on my turf. He was delicious.

What became this pike's downfall was his unwillingness to let go. It became a metaphor for me when my plan or approach is not working. Sometimes you have to let go of something you desperately want. This may seem to fly in the face of the quality of persistence. But it's more about being persistent while being intelligent and flexible. Persistence without situational awareness can lead to downfall. Blindly hanging on to a way of doing something just because that is the way we have always done it can be harmful to our health. Be flexible. Let go. Try a new approach that may work. Don't become someone's dinner.

Chapter Eighteen
Resiliency Factor: Self-Discipline

"Without self-discipline, success is impossible, period."
Lou Holtz, football coach, Notre Dame (Retired)

Self-discipline requires inner fortitude, which requires consistent development. Your parents start establishing boundaries for you from infancy. This continues through childhood as you grow, until you leave for the great big world beyond those walls of your home. Those boundaries are meant to keep you safe and protected until you reach a point where you gain the strength to discipline yourself. You typically mimic your parental role models, siblings, or other influential figures from your youth. Your teachers, coaches, heroes, classmates, and idols all play a part in establishing your personal level of self-discipline.

Life experiences and events also serve as mentors, teaching you lessons, what works, and what it takes to move on. The

Lou Holtz quote at the beginning of this chapter is worthy of consideration and, more importantly, application to our daily situations. Success and self-discipline are intricately tied together. Self-discipline and self-sacrifice set the stage for success.

In his sophomore year of high school, Michael Jordan was denied an opportunity to play basketball. He did not let that stop him from pursuing his goal. He kept practicing, perfecting his skills until he made it on the team. His father had this to say about Michael Jordan's competitive nature: "What he [Michael Jordan] does have is a competition problem. He was born with that...the person he tries to outdo most of the time is himself."[47]

Jordan became one of the greatest basketball players of all time. He led the Bulls to six national championships and earned the NBA Most Valuable Player Award five times. His success came as a result of the self-confidence that he built up. He accomplished this through a disciplined regimen that allowed him to accomplish his personal goal of playing in every game and playing well. Remember the old adage, "Practice makes perfect"? Well, that's the philosophy that individuals who are self-disciplined use to train their bodies, minds, and spirits to perform a certain way.

Courage to maintain a high degree of self-control comes from your belief system. Self-discipline helps you to follow your values, and your personal moral compass empowers you to stay the course, even in the difficult moments. You might define success as a work promotion, being proficient in the sport of your choice, or being a great wife or husband. Self-

47) Michael Jordan. (n.d.). Retrieved January 28, 2015, from http://www.biography.com/people/michael-jordan-9358066#synopsis.

discipline helps you consistently take small, daily actions to move you closer to your goal.

Now let's take a look at why self-discipline is important to resiliency. Self-discipline is what it takes to consistently implement your plan of action. On January 1, many people decide to go on weight-loss programs for the New Year. Then, by the second week of February, about 80% of those people have slacked off or stopped altogether. They lacked the self-discipline to follow through with the daily actions that would have given them significant results.

Here are some tips to stay on track with self-control:

- OWN IT: Accept ownership for your behavior. Stop blaming others; step up and take responsibility for your actions.

- LEAN INTO PAIN: Do the thing that you are putting off. Push yourself to start the task. Then, regardless of how unpleasant it is in the beginning, usually you will begin to enjoy it. As you gain momentum taking action, you'll feel more encouraged to keep it up and accomplish your next milestone. This will build self-control like a muscle.

- BE PROACTIVE: Try to anticipate problems before they slow you down. Decide what you are going to do when facing a choice or moral dilemma. Knowing in advance what you are going to do when facing a problem can help you avoid a poor decision when you are emotionally depleted.

- BE RATIONAL: Don't be impulsive with major decisions. Think about the consequences. Think about the impact of your actions on your future self. Learn to put some space between desire and decision.

WHY DOES SELF-DISCIPLINE INCREASE RESILIENCY?

In studying research on the various resiliency factors, I have found that the reasons most of these factors increase resilience are pretty straightforward. It makes sense at first blush that having a good support system in the form of a loving family would help you get through challenges. It's obvious that if you have a sense of humor and meditate and work out, you will be better off when dealing with stress.

However, some of the factors are less obvious. I read Dr. Robert Brooks' research stating that self-discipline is a vital component of a resilient mindset. I wondered, what is it about self-discipline that makes us more stress-resilient? The answer didn't hit me right away.

As I read a little more of Dr. Brooks' work, I saw the connections between stress and lack of self-control. If you are too impulsive or compulsive, you will invite stress into your life. Typically impulsive people have trouble controlling appetites, and give in to temptations such as inappropriate sex, pornography addictions, overeating, drugs, alcohol, losing their temper, and other issues. Those behaviors cause stress.

In addition, they are usually behaviors that compromise our values, so we feel guilt and shame, which only serves to magnify the stress.

I figured that self-discipline is not as much a characteristic that builds personal resilience as it is a characteristic that helps us avoid the stress in the first place.

However, as I studied a little more about the brain and how it works, I made some new connections. Generally speaking, our prefrontal cortex is the rational, reasoning, and logical part of our brain. Our amygdala and the rest of our limbic system are the emotional and animalistic parts of our brain. The limbic system is responsible for our "fight or flight" response. When you give in to temptation by doing something that is pleasurable, even though you know it is wrong, it is your limbic system winning out over your prefrontal cortex. When you do something that is hard, like writing a presentation when it would be easier to watch TV, that's your prefrontal cortex winning out over your limbic system. But when you quit writing before you are done to go watch the latest episode of Game of Thrones, you guessed it: the limbic system is back in charge.

What does this have to do with resiliency? Worry, fear, and anxiety are based in the limbic system. Most worries and fears are not rational. The prefrontal cortex knows that flying is statistically safer than driving, yet the limbic system causes many people to be stressed every time they step on a plane.

Which do you give more weight to: your prefrontal cortex or your limbic system?

People with a high level of self-discipline are people who likely have a stronger prefrontal cortex, and rely more on logic and reasoning. They would tend not to be influenced by irrational fears. Their rational brain would win out over the emotional brain more often than not. Now it makes more sense to me why people who are self-disciplined would be resistant to negative stress reactions.

Yes, this is oversimplifying a complex relationship between parts of the brain, but the generalization works. It works because we just need to know the basics so we can improve our odds in this constant mental battle.

Self-discipline is like a muscle. It will be built and strengthened over time as you practice resisting temptation and are proactive with goals. It doesn't happen overnight, but as you exercise your self-control it will grow. Another method to improve in this area is meditation. Research has shown that meditation increases self-discipline, makes people less impulsive, and makes them more likely to think through their problems instead of reacting emotionally.

As you reach higher levels of self-discipline, you will avoid bringing a lot of stress into your life, and the unavoidable stress will not crush you.

CHAPTER NINETEEN
RESILIENCY FACTOR: CREATIVITY

"Children are happy because they don't have a file in their minds called 'All the Things That Could Go Wrong.'"
Marianne Williamson

Creativity is a powerful tool that releases a soul bound to a crisis or tragedy. Children are the best example of this form of resiliency. The creativity of toddlers is not bound by the opinions of others or a need to please them, unless it's their parents. One minute they may be fighting on the playground over a chalk-drawn masterpiece, and the next they are sharing the credit because of a little prompting by a teacher. Toddlers more often fight for the right to create and own what they've created. No one has told them not to create, or that their skills are inadequate to do it well. They proceed until they hit a major stumbling block, usually delivered by a playground peer or a well-meaning adult. In terms of resiliency, I encourage you to return to that time where your creativity was free-flowing and unhindered.

Journaling is the way I use creativity to build resilience. Seeing my words come together before my eyes brings clarity and strength. I am better able to evaluate a situation that I've drawn out of self and put on paper. I see my life differently, looking down from above the situation. This perspective makes it easier to move the pieces around, constructing a clearer picture to get a more ideal outcome.

Megan Van Meter at ABCs for Therapists had this to say about creativity and resiliency: "Responding to new threats and challenges with adaptive and inventive solutions is how the human brain problem-solves its way beyond those threats and challenges in order to thrive. Face it; if we only encountered the same old threats and challenges, they wouldn't really be threats and challenges—we'd already have formulas in place for managing them. But when we're confronted with the unfamiliar, the unthinkable, the unimaginable, we have nothing to fall back on but our ability to innovate and improvise."[48]

Creativity increases resiliency through outlets such as art therapy, dramatic arts, and journaling. Writing has been shown to be an effective method for treating the stress response after disaster. But there is also some research showing that it is protective, and builds resiliency. Dr. Frederic Flach says, "Learning to acquire and practice proven methods of stimulating creativity will substantially enhance our resources to cope with stress." When we do art in whatever form, journaling, writing poetry, we access parts of our minds and emotions that we may not otherwise access on a daily basis. When we

48) Van Meter, M. (n.d.). Creativity and Resilience. Retrieved January 28, 2015, from http://abcsfortherapists.com/creativity-and-resilience/.

reach deeply into ourselves, we may find bastions of strength, or find meaning in some far part of our soul that we wouldn't have found without being creative. We may tap into a powerful part of our subconscious mind that has been dormant for too long.

According to Al Seibert, Ph.D. the least creative people tend to be very judgmental and stuck in habitual ways of thinking. Open-minded people are more curious, and are not limited by as many opinions or judgments. Creative people are open to a wider variety of solutions, and hence do better during crisis or disaster. On a more practical level, creative people are better at creative problem solving, and adapting to unfamiliar situations, stepping outside the boundaries of old ways of thinking. Creativity can be learned as we apply ourselves to creative pursuits.

Let's take a look at some modern-day creative thinkers in the business arena: Steve Jobs (Apple and Pixar), Richard Branson (Virgin), and Jeff Bezos (Amazon). Progress is often defined by major creative thinkers or innovative movements that improve people's overall quality of life. These creative thinkers are massive wealth builders. Each of these men created their own paradigm and maintained their course in the midst of major opposition and controversy. Since the beginning of time, there has always been someone who's said, "We don't do it that way around here." These three men ignored the critics when those people tried to convince them to do otherwise. History clearly chronicles the great battles of the naysayers and the innovators. History usually vindicates the creators and innovators, but even when it doesn't exonerate them, they derived benefit anyway, because the vision driving them also made them resilient to the challenges they faced.

If you need an innovative strategy to bounce back from some trauma or obstacle in your life, you have the innate power to find the solution through unleashing your creativity. Choose a method that best suits you and create a better life for yourself: on the pages of a journal, in front of a blank canvas, or through interpretive dance! There is more in you than what has happened to you. Use your creativity when circumstances overwhelm you. Return to that state of creativity and flow that you had as a child.

When I was in Israel, I attended Parent's Place in Sderot, which is the Israeli town I referred to in a previous chapter, on the border of the Gaza Strip. Over a third of the children in Sderot had symptoms of PTSD due to the thousands of Kassam rockets that have rained down on their town over the last several years. As I mentioned earlier, the Israel Center for the Treatment of Psychotrauma (ICTP) started a program at the Parent's Place. They found that creativity and play seemed to be two of the first victims of the terror. When your town is under attack, and you are worried for your children's safety, you tend not to remember to play with them. So the ICTP program reintroduced creativity and play in a safe location. (The building is bombproof.) Free imaginative play is a central tool for cognitive, emotional, and social development for all children. Play is a central and effective tool in promoting resilience for children undergoing traumatic events and living in conditions of crisis. The program incorporates music, crafts, drama, and art. The program has been effective in reducing negative outcomes for the children.

After going through trauma, creativity is probably the last thing you want to think about. But at the very least, write about what happened. Getting your thoughts down on paper has an amazing effect on releasing stress. Also remember play is not only for children. Adults need to take time to play. We don't always do it, but it is healthy for our minds and souls.

CHAPTER TWENTY

RESILIENCY FACTOR: LIVE IN THE NOW

"It doesn't matter whether this is the worst time
to be alive or the best, whether you're in a good job market
or a bad one, or that the obstacle you face is intimidating or
burdensome. What matters right now is right now."
Ryan Holiday, The Obstacle Is the Way

Living in the now is the opposite of being stuck in the past. For example, constantly longing for a pre-vious time in your life or being held captive by a past event. You can probably think of someone who lives in the good ol' days, still wearing the clothes and mindset of a forgotten era. Studies have found that people who live in the past don't react as well in disasters as people who live in the now.

Some people are future-tense thinkers, and that is okay, as long as you believe the future is going to be positive, and you're not a worrier. If you have anxiety about the future, and think the economy will never recover and the polar bears are all going to drown soon, then that's not helpful either.

A group of people doing extremely well at living in the now, not dwelling on the past, are Buddhist monks. There is a Zen Master who tells a story of two monks walking along a path. It goes something like this:

Once there were two monks walking along a path through the woods. They came to a stream and encountered a young woman dressed in fine silks, unable to cross the stream without ruining her clothes. One of the monks offered to carry her on his back. She climbed on. They all crossed the stream. On the other side he set her down. She thanked him and went on her way. The two monks continued walking. The monastery to which these monks belonged had a rule prohibiting them from touching women. The other monk was horrified that his brother in the order had broken this rule, and was agonizing about it as they walked. He thought, "How could he violate his vows like this? Will he confess? Should I tell the abbot? Will they throw him out? Will I get in trouble too? Why did he put me in this situation?" And he got more and more upset as he ruminated on it.

Finally, after they had walked about a mile, he stopped and shouted, "How could you do that?"

"Do what?" asked the first monk.

"How could you touch that woman?"

"Oh, her? I set her down when we got across the stream. Why, my brother, are you still carrying her on your back?"

Choosing to live in the now, versus living in the past or in the future, is a critical part of resiliency. Here are some suggestions on how to live in the now from the National Institutes of Health, part of the U.S. Department of Health and Human Services:

BEING MINDFUL

The concept of mindfulness is simple, but becoming a more mindful person requires commitment and practice. Here are some tips to help you get started:

- Take some deep breaths. Breathe in through your nose to a count of 4, hold for 1 second and then exhale through the mouth to a count of 5. Repeat often.

- Enjoy a stroll. As you walk, notice your breath and the sights and sounds around you. As thoughts and worries enter your mind, note them but then return to the present.

- Practice mindful eating. Be aware of taste, textures and flavors in each bite, and listen to your body when you are hungry and full.

- Find mindfulness resources in your local community, including yoga and meditation classes, mindfulness-based stress reduction programs and books.[49]

Other Resources for Mindfulness:

- Free Guided Meditations from UCLA Health at http://bit.ly/LKnnua

- The Free Mindfulness Project at http://www.freemindfulness.org/download

MINDFULNESS

Mindfulness is moment-by-moment awareness. Attentively observing your experience as it unfolds. Paying attention without judgment or evaluation. It's empty of comparing, assessing, judging, and commentary. It involves a high degree of openness, receptivity, and inquisitiveness. It's directing and maintaining non-judgmental attention to the experience of our bodies and minds in the present moment.

Mindfulness helps you understand the world and yourself more clearly. Too often we live according to habit or routine without making a conscious choice. Mindfulness teaches there are many things in the world over which we have no control. However, we can control our mind, our experience, and our perspective. I can't change the past, but I can decide how the past will influence the person I am now. We can be more deliberate in how we allow uncontrollable events to affect us.

---

49) Mindfulness Matters. (2012, January 1). Retrieved from National Institutes of Health, part of the U.S. Department of Health and Human Services.

In Robert Sapolsky's book *Why Zebras Don't Get Ulcers,* he says that animals don't get chronic stress. When a zebra runs from a lion, its cortisol levels go down afterwards. The zebra goes back to feeding, not wondering when the lion might chase it again, or theorizing about why the lion chased it in the first place. Why not some other zebra? It's not fair. Humans keep the stress going because of thought and emotion. Only humans can be stressed from things that exist in idea only, like being stressed because we are remembering a past argument. We can learn something from the zebras by letting go of stuff from our past and living in the now!

THE SEDONA METHOD

This method was developed by Lester Levenson and made popular by Hale Dwoskin in the book *The Sedona Method.* Essentially, it's just all about letting go. Letting go of negative feelings and emotions, guilt or resentment from the past. Letting go of worries and expectations about the future. Just mentally releasing emotions that don't serve us. I don't have enough space to teach the method here, so buy Hale's book. Just a teaser of the way it works is, you ask yourself questions about whatever is stressing you, such as "Could I let this feeling go?" "Would I let it go?" "When would I let it go?" "Can I let it go now?" It's a cognitive exercise that seems very simple but it can have a powerful impact.

I've lent the book to several women I know: my mother, my ex, and my girlfriend. Of course, it was self-serving because usually I want them to let go of something that I did wrong. I find the women in my life have the best memories when it comes to holding on to something that I said that they perceived as offensive, even if it was years before. They even remember what I was wearing at the time, and where we were, and the song that was playing on the radio. I tell them they need the Sedona Method. Yes, I was being a jerk and recommending it for the wrong reason, just because I wanted to be absolved. But truly we all need the book. We all need to be able to let go of those things that take up space in our heads and cause us pain for way too long.

LIVE IN THE NOW

As I mentioned, people who live in the present moment handle stress and trauma better than those who dwell on the past or are preoccupied with the future. If you feel anxiety, worry, or shame, chances are you are either ruminating on the past or worried about some future possibility. Either way, it's not helpful. You can't change the past, and most of what you worry about in the future will never happen.

Of course, you already know that on an intellectual level, but it's not so easy to change. We are emotional beings driven by subconscious minds. Is it possible to change, and to release the anxiety and other feelings that cause stress? Yes. Mindfulness meditation has been shown to reduce stress, anxiety, and depression, and also increase creativity and energy. Monks who practice mindfulness regularly have high levels of equanimity and well-being. Mindfulness meditation is focusing on your breathing, or one of your senses, or your body and how it feels, or even an awareness of your current thoughts. Choose one of those to pay attention to. Start with meditating on inhaling and exhaling, excluding all other thoughts. It takes practice, but with practice you will gain an increased ability to pay attention to only breathing.

Focus your awareness on the here and now. Pay attention to whatever you are doing. If your mind wanders, bring it back. Be aware of your emotions and feelings, but learn to accept them. Be aware of your feelings from a third-person perspective, as if from outside of yourself. This helps you to be non-judgmental and non-reactive so you can respond better to whatever situation you may be in.

When you are feeling stressed, examine your thoughts. In most cases you are not stressed about something in the present moment. You are worried about something in the future that may or may not happen. Or you are upset about something that has already happened. You may feel guilt, shame, anger, or hurt. If you bring your thoughts to the present moment it will reduce stress, because things are rarely as bad in the present moment as our thoughts about the past or future are.

For example: When I was going through a separation after 18 years of marriage, I was hurt because it came as a surprise to me. I found myself ruminating and feeling sorry for myself whenever I had time alone with my feelings. I had an hour-long commute to work, so as I drove my thoughts were on "What went wrong?" "How could she leave me?". But when

I caught myself and brought my thoughts back to the present moment, it didn't hurt as much. I would think, "Whether she left me or not, I would still be driving this car to work right now." That precise moment was the same, whether we were together or not. That moment was not different than during my commute a year before or five years before. I thought, "In this moment there is no stress."

Don't dwell on the past, which you can't change, or feel anxiety for the future that you can't control. Live in the present moment.

CHAPTER TWENTY-ONE
RESILIENCY FACTOR: INTELLIGENCE

"Strenuous intellectual work and the study of
God's Nature are the angels that will lead me through
all the troubles of this life with consolation, strength,
and uncompromising rigor."
Albert Einstein

In 1991 Albert Einstein was declared TIME magazine's "Person of the Century." His "intellect, coupled his strong passion for social justice and dedication to pacifism, left the world with infinite knowledge and pioneering moral leadership."[50] It was evident at an early age that Einstein was brilliant, but he wasn't a man without personal suffering or tragedy. We can assume that he used his intelligence to maneuver the troubles of this life.

The American Psychological Association says that, "intelligence refers to intellectual functioning. Intelligence quotients, or IQ tests, compare your performance with other

---

50) Albert Einstein. (n.d.). Retrieved January 29, 2015, from http://einstein.biz/biography.php.

people your age who take the same test. These tests don't measure all kinds of intelligence, however. For example, such tests can't identify differences in social intelligence, the expertise people bring to their interactions with others. There are also generational differences in the population as a whole. Better nutrition, more education and other factors have resulted in IQ improvements for each generation."[51]

Research shows that higher intelligence equals higher resiliency. A more intelligent individual possesses better decision-making skills in difficult circumstances. Studies in the U.S. Military show people with higher intellectual intelligence and social intelligence, and higher education, have lower rates of PTSD.

THE BRAIN CYCLE

The brain is designed to take stress in 30-second bursts. For example, when our ancestors got chased by a saber-toothed tiger, it implemented the fight or flight sequence, which allowed them to respond to that urgent situation. However, your brain is not designed for the chronic stress you feel every day due to a bad boss. That stress causes problems at the neuronal level in the brain. The result is that stressed brains do not learn. And therein is the cycle, because lower intelligence equals lower ability to deal with stress. So you make poor decisions because you're stressed and you're not learning, and the poor decisions cause even more stress, causing an even more negative impact on the brain.

51) Intelligence. (n.d.). Retrieved January 29, 2015, from http://apa.org/topics/intelligence/index.aspx.

Dr. Bill McDermott told me about a guy he talked to at Ground Zero who saved himself and others because he was intelligent and knew how to apply his acumen. He was a construction worker who was on the 18th floor and he brought 70 people out with him. Even though it was dark and full of smoke, because he was smart, he had a template of the floorplan in his head. He knew what to do in the smoke (to stay low) and he got people out. He survived and helped others survive. He integrated the knowledge he had compiled over the years, brought it all together when he needed it, and had grace and problem-solving ability under pressure.

"Intellectual ability may be a protective factor for several reasons. It may allow individuals to better (1) comprehend their symptoms, (2) express themselves when talking about their symptoms, and (3) engage in flexible and creative problem solving." [52]

Put in a slightly more crass way, "Life is tough; it's tougher when you're stupid." (John Wayne in *The Sands of Iwo Jima*.)

I know we don't have as much control over this factor as most of the other factors, but we still have some control over whether we take our innate social and intellectual intelligence and either enhance it or diminish it.

When I was taking a resiliency course at the Hebrew University of Jerusalem, one exercise gave me insight into how some people enhance their intellectual ability when stressed, and how this could lead to better outcomes. The course was about applying different coping mechanisms to stress, and how it's helpful to increase your repertoire of coping skills to

52) Lukey, B. (2008). *Biobehavioral resilience to stress.* Boca Raton: CRC Press.

increase overall resiliency.

We had to write down on a 3x5 card an activity that we used to cope, and write why it helped us cope. Then we had to find a partner who didn't use that method to cope. I teamed up with Stephen. My method was a sense of humor, being able to find humor in difficult situations. Stephen didn't use this method to cope, so I explained to him how it worked for me. Then Stephen shared his method of coping, which was through intellectual pursuit, like taking courses. That wasn't a method I had ever used to deal with stress. In fact, I always thought of courses and other intellectual pursuits as causing a certain amount of stress. He explained how it worked for him.

Stephen is an orthopedic surgeon and has very high demands in his workplace. He told me that when the pressure gets to him, he likes to read or take courses on a subject unrelated to his work. He finds that it relaxes him, while at the same time providing growth and enhancing his mind. As part of this exercise he had to commit to use my method and I had to commit to use his method. Then we would each have one more coping mechanism in our personal repertoire.

It's clear to see that a guy like Stephen would come up with better solution-focused ways to solve problems or bypass obstacles than someone who just uses alcohol to deal with stress. This is a factor that resonates with my son. Ryan is fourteen, but he knows more about world geography, politics and history, than most adults. He loves to read and is very rational. I can see that his perspective of problems is less emotional and more intellectual. His matter-of-fact attitude helps him dismiss troubles that would cause other teens to react. Even if you don't think of yourself as an intellectual person, you can find something that you enjoy learning about. By using critical thinking skills to view life's problems instead of your emotional mind, you will reduce your stress. Enhance your mind and you enhance your resiliency.

Chapter Twenty-Two
Resiliency Factor: Forgiveness

"Forgiveness is an act of the will, and the will can function regardless of the temperature of the heart."
Corrie ten Boom

Corrie ten Boom, author of *The Hiding Place*, along with her family members, helped Jews escape the Nazi Holocaust during World War II. They were imprisoned for it. It may seem strange that a woman who had witnessed the atrocities of war would say this about forgiveness, but she recognized the pit that lack of forgiveness could trap people in. Forgiveness is not a gift that you give others, it is a gift you give yourself.

Dr. Roberta Greene, a University of Texas at Austin scholar, studies resiliency in individuals who have the capacity to bounce back after grave traumas and major catastrophes. She chose to study Holocaust survivors. The article *Forgiveness*

Illuminated had this to say about her findings: "What Greene found amazed her. She discovered that despite experiencing earlier extraordinary horror, many Holocaust survivors were resilient adults. They had taken action to make new lives out of the pain of the past. Lived with it, accepted it and as one survivor said, 'go on, and go on and go on.'"[53]

Whatever you may have experienced that shattered your world view and damaged your soul has the potential to hold you stagnant in that place of pain for a lifetime. Resilient people choose to forgive because it frees them to concentrate on moving on with their lives. You must forgive to move forward. Don't get stuck in the past.

Lyn Worsley, in the blog *Forgiveness and Resilience*, had this to say about the forgiveness process:

"So if someone does something wrong to you, you have a reaction to that which is equal to what has been done to you. This reaction, however, can come in many forms. You can be a victim where you feel wronged and helpless and experience depression, or you can react with indignation and anger. Both of these reactions not only equal the trauma or the hurtful event but can double the pain and the effect on those traumatized. So the action of the trauma or hurt has an equal reaction of hurt or anger. However, there is another way and that is to be proactive in response to the trauma. Forgiveness is not doing nothing, because that will end up with either an eventual victim or vindictive reaction. Forgiveness is to respond to the trauma in a direction that is more helpful for everyone.

---

53) Forgiveness Illuminated. (n.d.). Retrieved January 30, 2015, from http://www.utexas.edu/features/2009/04/20/forgiveness/.

A proactive response is taking the steps toward a more positive future regardless of the hurt inside.

A proactive response is sometimes doing the opposite to what you feel like doing. It can change how you feel about the event. It can channel the energy towards a different goal. Real forgiveness does that. It channels the energy where it belongs and it is neither seeking revenge nor being a doormat."[54]

A while back I had an ongoing conflict with a coworker. It seems to happen to everyone at some point. I felt that this person was working to undermine me, and they also put in a formal complaint about me. It wasn't easy, but I chose to forgive that person, to let go of the grudge and the hard feelings. I had to release this negative energy that I was carrying around with me, for my own good. Imagine carrying an extra 50 lbs. around with you every day. Navigating a poisonous workplace can make you feel like you have that extra weight on your shoulders. It makes your environment very uncomfortable. But you can't expect everyone else to fix it for you. So I let go of it. Now we can work together with no stress because we both chose to forgive each other, and repair that bridge that had been burned. I've seen other people in my workplace carry grudges for years, even decades. It's just not worth the stress.

I recently read an article, *Managing Yourself, An Antidote to Incivility*, in the April 2016 issue of Harvard Business Review. The author, Christine Porath, quoted some statistics from her workplace conflict surveys that found 85% of people are unsatisfied with the results of confronting the person that they

54) Forgiveness and Resilience. (2013, April 15). Retrieved January 30, 2015, from http://www.theresiliencecentre.com.au/blog/forgiveness-and-resilience/.

have conflict with. Also 85% of people were unsatisfied with the result when they tried to avoid the person. Finally, 85% were not satisfied with the result of institutional remedies, such as mediation. So—what's the answer? Porath's position is that the only option is building resilience so that you can thrive despite workplace conflict. I agree. It also made me wonder, "Why are workplace conflict remedies so ineffective?" I believe a major reason is because people won't forgive and let go.

FORGIVING YOURSELF

You also need to forgive yourself. When I do presentations I usually talk about the stress inflicted on us, such as trauma, unexpected changes in our circumstances, or even high demands that are placed on us at work. But what about stress and anxiety we cause ourselves because we messed up?

I often talk to people who have stress in their lives because of mistakes they have made, errors in judgment, or not doing what they knew was the right thing to do. This feeling of guilt can be a powerful negative emotion that can harm our ability to be happy, effective, and successful. So you need to let it go.

But hang on, aren't we supposed to feel guilty when we do something wrong? Absolutely. There is a valid purpose for guilt. It is to let us know we violated our standards; we did something that was not consistent with our values, with who we are. We need to use that horrible feeling as an impetus to change. Guilt should be used as a course correction, not a reason to beat yourself up for the next five years. Too often people feel guilt for so long that it changes their perception of themselves, and it turns into shame and self-hatred. That type of emotion is not helpful, and it decreases the person's ability to deal with any type of stress.

We all make mistakes, but feeling endless shame and guilt is not productive. When you mess up, use the guilt as an impelling force to propel positive changes, and then forgive yourself and *let it go*.

CHAPTER TWENTY-THREE
RESILIENCY FACTOR: LOVE, COMPASSION, AND GRATITUDE

"When you arise in the morning, think of
what a precious privilege it is to be alive—to breathe,
to think, to enjoy, to love."
Marcus Aurelius

Social science research has shown that altruism is associated with resilience, positive mental health, and well-being.[55] All three of these altruistic values—love, compassion, and gratitude—are major contributors to resilience and rebuilding your life after a tragedy or crisis. These "feel good," emotions are not out of reach during adversity. But they take effort and willpower to evoke. They are major combatants when it comes to eliminating fear and stress and other negative feelings that inhibit thriving. Love increases the biochemical oxytocin, which is a natural stress reliever.

55) Southwick, S. & Charney, D. (2012) *Resilience: The Science of Mastering Life's Greatest Challenges.* Cambridge University Press.

We talked earlier about the importance of loving relationships and family in relation to your immediate support system as you suffer emotionally. Showing love and compassion towards people outside of your support system, who are perhaps less fortunate than you, can also facilitate growing resiliency in your life. Don't discount your ability to give love and show compassion during a crisis. Numerous stories of "Good Samaritans" came out after the 9/11 attacks. Police, firefighters, and medical personnel all went to the scene of the Twin Towers knowing that there was a chance that they would not return. Their true compassion for others compelled them to go to the rescue of complete strangers. Geraldine Brooks is quoted as saying, "September 11, 2001, revealed heroism in ordinary people who might have gone through their lives never called upon to demonstrate the extent of their courage."

Giving to others has been cited as a possible antidote to the negative effects of stress. A study lead by author Michael J. Poulin of the University of Buffalo indicates that it may be a viable remedy for stress. Poulin and his team interviewed approximately 850 people, ages 34-93, who were living in Detroit, Michigan. Participants were asked to report stressful events they had encountered in the past year and how much they helped others during that time. Deaths that occurred within the group during the next five years were tracked using obituaries and public death records. They found that every major stressful event increased an individual's risk of death by 30%. Yet this increase was reduced considerably for those who reported high rates of helping others while dealing with a lot of stress. The evidence suggests that giving to others reduces stress-induced mortality.[56]

Can you find the courage to look within and show true compassion for someone else during your time of need? I say yes, you can, because loving others and being moved by compassion for them is as much a part of the human condition as tragedy.

WHAT DOES NEUROSCIENCE HAVE TO SAY ABOUT THIS?

In the article *The Neuroscience of Resiliency: An Interview with Linda Graham*, Dr. Elisha Goldstein asked Linda Graham to share some of her practices from her book, *Bouncing Back: Rewiring Your Brain for Maximum Resilience and Well-Being,* to help us wire a more resilient brain. Graham responded: "The brain becomes more resilient any time we steadily cultivate the positive, pro-social emotions like gratitude, kindness, compassion, serenity, awe, delight, love. Twenty years of positive psychology research and twenty years of neuroscience research are converging in their discoveries that a daily gratitude practice antidotes the innate negativity bias of the brain. For our survival our brains are hard-wired to pay more attention to negative and intense experiences than positive and subtle ones. That negativity bias is how we survive as individuals and as a species; we are never going to not do that. But when we intentionally and steadily cultivate a practice of gratitude for

---

56) Stress as a positive: Recent research that suggests it has benefits. (2013, September 4). Retrieved January 30, 2015, from http://blog.ted.com/2013/09/04/could-stress-be-good-for-you-recent-research-that-suggests-it-has-benefits/.

the people and processes that sustain our life, we expand our perception of our experience back out of a narrow, contracted, survival mode—fight-flight-freeze-numb out-collapse—to a more expansive, more optimistic perspective, where we can again discern options and possibilities. Resilience is a reliably measurable outcome of cultivating positive emotions such as gratitude."[57]

MORE ON GRATITUDE

Gratitude is the quality of being thankful for something and being willing to acknowledge your attitude of appreciation, even if only to yourself. Sometimes it's very difficult to find something to be grateful about in the midst of a trial or tribulation, but it's not impossible. Ask yourself positive questions, like "Who am I grateful for?" and "What am I grateful for?" Below is a list of 31 reasons to be grateful no matter where you may find yourself in life:

1. Gratitude makes us happier.

2. Gratitude makes people like us.

3. Gratitude makes us healthier.

4. Gratitude boosts our career.

5. Gratitude strengthens our emotions.

6. Gratitude develops our personality.

7. Gratitude makes us more optimistic.

---

57) The Neuroscience of Resiliency: An Interview with Linda Graham. (n.d.). Retrieved January 30, 2015, from http://blogs.psychcentral.com/mindfulness/2014/04/the-neuroscience-of-resiliency-an-interview-with-linda-graham/.

8. Gratitude reduces materialism.

9. Gratitude increases spiritualism.

10. Gratitude makes us less self-centered.

11. Gratitude increases self-esteem.

12. Gratitude improves our sleep.

13. Gratitude keeps us away from the doctor.

14. Gratitude lets us live longer.

15. Gratitude increases our energy levels.

16. Gratitude makes us more likely to exercise.

17. Gratitude helps us bounce back.

18. Gratitude makes us feel good.

19. Gratitude makes our memories happier.

20. Gratitude reduces feelings of envy.

21. Gratitude helps us relax.

22. Gratitude makes us friendlier.

23. Gratitude helps our marriages.

24. Gratitude makes us look good.

25. Gratitude helps us make friends.

26. Gratitude deepens friendships.

27. Gratitude makes us more effective managers.

28. Gratitude helps us network.

29. Gratitude increases our goal achievement.

30. Gratitude improves our decision making.

31. Gratitude increases our productivity.[58]

I'm sure out of this list, you will be able to find at least one reason to compel you to work on feeling gratitude. Dr. Martin Seligman recommends doing his "Three Good Things" exercise every night. I admit I don't do it every night, but I do sometimes. The exercise is simple: write down three things that you are grateful for. This changes your perspective over time to focus on the good in the world and increases resiliency. It has taught me to focus on what I am grateful for, and as a result I would find more things to be grateful for each day. You get whatever you focus on in life and focusing on gratefulness increases your capacity for dealing with stress.

COMPASSION IN THE WORKPLACE

I recently spoke at a conference where the audience was fun, positive, and energetic. You'd never guess that they are managers in an agency that is dealing on a daily basis with details of horrible trauma. And because they are managers, they are stuck in the middle between the front-line employees and the executive level, which (as anyone who has been in mid-level management can tell you) is a lonely job. There is a high level of organizational stress because of trying to juggle many competing demands from caseload to administration, and from

58) The 31 Benefits of Gratitude You Didn't Know About: How Gratitude Can Change Your Life. (n.d.). Retrieved January 30, 2015, from http://happierhuman.com/benefits-of-gratitude/.

managing human resources to dealing with external agencies that sometimes work at cross-purposes.

Being the only manager in a satellite office magnifies the sense of being alone and feeling a lack of support at times. That's why this conference was so healthy and positive for these managers. It gave them an opportunity to network with other people who are in the same boat. The theme of the conference was *Resiliency*, and I really believe it boosted the resiliency of the already very resilient group. Despite the conference theme, I think the part that provided the most value was the networking. Not because they needed to trade best practices, but because it was an opportunity for them to have compassion for each other. The managers, who were normally on their own, now had a group of peers who understood exactly what they were going through. That is often better than a professional counselor. These managers, who were almost all women, really got each other. They were able to vent and have their feelings validated by others who knew exactly what they were talking about. This is extremely healthy. Despite the negativity of the work they are involved with, this group of managers showed compassion and caring for each other, and expressed gratitude for the positive outcomes they had in their communities. While listening to their conversations I was impressed with their compassion for their employees and clients, too. I know that is one reason they were resilient.

Dr. Robert Brooks in *The Power of Resilience* says, "Many articles have been written describing the emergence of a 'helper's high', an exhilarating feeling rooted in both physical and emotional changes after showing compassion or helping others. When people display compassion, not only do they enhance their resilience by connecting with others, but they also nurture the belief that they make a positive difference in their world."

These women were clearly making a positive difference in the world and they were protecting their minds with their altruistic values.

What can you do to increase love, compassion, and gratitude in your life today?

CHAPTER TWENTY-FOUR
RESILIENCY FACTOR:
PERCEPTION OF PROBLEMS

"Change the way you look at things
and the things you look at change."
Wayne W. Dyer

There is no objective reality with stress. It's all about how you perceive the problem. The same problem to two different people can be a *challenge* for one person and a *catastrophe* for the other. The problem is the same, it's just that they had a different perception. Who do you think has more stress?

How do you keep a positive perception when facing life's problems? Make a positive appraisal of the situation, and minimize the catastrophic aspects of the situation. "Resilience has been associated with a tendency to perceive potentially stressful events in less threatening terms." (Tugade, 2004) Periodically perform a self-assessment of your overall view on life. Find a person with a positive perception and emulate them.

In our minds we can redefine a "crisis" as a "challenge." We can reframe stressors in a more positive light.

A few years ago Ryan, a member of my Emergency Response Team (ERT), was out on a snowmobile to rescue some overdue ice fishermen in the far north of Ontario. His snowmobile broke down and his partner went on without him to complete the rescue. His partner was unable to come back and get him as planned because the rescue of the ice fishermen took him much further away than anticipated. Ryan was stranded all night in minus-40-degree weather, with no survival equipment. The only thing that kept him alive was walking around the snowmobile all night, so he didn't freeze. It was a dangerous situation, and he could have died. A couple times he was close. He was exhausted, and twice he laid down and put his head back and was about to close his eyes, but he knew if he did he might never wake up. So he forced himself to get up and continued walking and running around the snowmobile.

At this time I was calling around to find a helicopter to rescue him. I was worried he wouldn't make it if we didn't get to him soon. But I couldn't find any helicopters up north that flew at night with instrumentation. So it wasn't until morning that a helicopter from a logging company could go find him. The helicopter went to rescue him in the morning, and when the door opened the first thing Ryan did was give two thumbs up and yell "ERT rules!!" He was happy and in good spirits and laughing about it. Some people placed in that circumstance would walk around the snowmobile all night thinking, "I'm going to die. I'm not going to make it." They might blame somebody. "I can't believe the police force put me in this situation. They killed me!" They might be having thoughts of self-blame, "I can't believe how stupid I am for not bringing the survival kit. I'm gonna die." What would you have been thinking all night?

I spoke to Ryan afterward and asked him what he was thinking. He told me he was walking around the snowmobile all night thinking, "This is easy overtime."

We both laughed about that. It's not the situation that determines your level of stress. It's how you frame it in your mind.

> *"If you are distressed by anything external, the pain is not due to the thing itself, but to your estimate of it; and this you have the power to revoke at any moment." – Marcus Aurelius, Meditations*

You will never know what's good and what's bad, anyway. Our perceptions can lie, or can be completely inaccurate because we don't know how our story ends. Here's a Zen story that emphasizes this point.

> *Long ago, there was an old farmer living on the outskirts of a little village. He was quite poor, possessing only a small piece of land, a small house in which he lived with his only son, and one horse.*
>
> *One day, the horse broke out of the corral and ran away. The neighbors came over to console the*

farmer. They said, "Oh, this is so terrible! You were poor before, but now you are destitute. What bad luck! This is the worst thing that could have happened."

The old farmer shrugged his shoulders and gently said, "Who knows what's good and what's bad?"

The farmer fixed the fence and left the gate open. The next day, his horse came back and went right into the corral, followed by a whole herd of wild horses. The neighbors came over to congratulate him. They said, "Oh, this is so wonderful! You were the poorest man in the village and now you're the richest. What good fortune! This is the best thing that could have happened."

The old farmer shrugged his shoulders and again said, "Who knows what's good and what's bad?"

The next day, his son was working to tame the new horses. One of them bucked and he fell off, breaking his leg. The neighbors came over and said, "Oh, this is so terrible! Now your son is hurt, the horses can't be tamed, and you have no one to help you harvest your crop. What bad luck! This is the worst thing that could have happened!"

The old farmer shrugged his shoulders and once more said, "Who knows what's good and what's bad?"

And the next day, the king's army came through the countryside, taking all the able-bodied young men off to battle, where they were almost sure to die. But because the old farmer's son's leg was hurt, he wasn't taken along. So who knows what's good and what's bad?

We often waste time with fantasies of how life should be, and "what if" this or that had happened. But it's healthier to think that something positive may come from whatever adversity we are facing. Either way we won't know, so we might as well think it will be something good as opposed to only bad coming from the situation. Perhaps you need to ask yourself, "Will this matter five years from now?" That should put things in a better perspective. I do that myself when I'm facing a difficult time. Or if it's a really big problem, ask yourself if it will matter as you are nearing the end of your life, and looking back on your experiences. You hold the paintbrush that colors the canvas of your life, especially after a tragedy. Your perception determines your experience, so choose the right colors.

MÁS SE PERDIÓ EN LA GUERRA

This is a Spanish expression that I would hear my wife saying when we were married. My ex grew up in Argentina and her father would say it to her when she was a kid. It translates to "More was lost in war." So, for example, Marisa would be walking down the street as a six-year-old in Buenos Aires and she would drop her ice cream cone on the ground. As she was about to cry at her lost ice cream, her father would say, "Más se perdió en la guerra." It's a reframing tool; it gives a different perspective. Yes, you lost your ice cream, but more was lost in war. You think you have it bad? You could have had your legs blown off by a land mine. It's extreme, but I always found it funny.

When we were going through our divorce after 18 years of marriage, I found out how much she would be getting from my police pension fund. Since I had been a cop for over 20 years at that time, it had added up. And since we were married most of that time, she was getting a big chunk of it. When I found out she would be getting over $300,000 from my pension fund, I was upset. I was worried about my own financial future and I was stressed because it was more than I thought she would be getting, and I was just angry. I called her and complained about how much she was taking and what it would do to me financially. She said, "Más se perdió en la guerra."

I started laughing. I'm actually laughing about it right now as I write this. Good reframe for me. More *was* lost in war.

PART THREE
RESILIENCY IS POWER

CHAPTER TWENTY-FIVE
FIVE-STEP FORMULA FOR STRESS IMMUNITY

"A kite rises highest against the wind, not with it"
Winston Churchill

In the previous chapters I've given you a lot of information. You know about all the various factors that will make you more resilient. But how do you apply it? That's always the hard part, actually putting your knowledge into practice. That was the hard part for me too. I had been teaching about resiliency factors for years, but when going through a rough patch I wasn't always good about applying my knowledge. I lived many of the resiliency factors, but there were others that I should have done better with. I knew there must be some way to put my knowledge into practice more effectively. Through research, experimentation, and consultation with psychologists I created a formula that makes it easier to apply resiliency factors during a time of struggle. This formula will help you handle the stress in your life, and help you build resiliency. It's called the *ADAPT to Succeed* Formula.

ADAPT TO SUCCEED FORMULA

The *ADAPT to Succeed* Formula is a five-step formula to guide you in your practice of resiliency while you are going through a stressful time. Using this formula can increase your capacity to deal with the stress immediately. I called it the *ADAPT to Succeed* Formula because ADAPT is an acronym for Accept, Decide, Apply a factor, Problem-focused response, and Take stock—the five steps to the formula, which I'll explain shortly. This formula brings success as it prevents you from being immobilized by fear or stuck in repetitive negative thoughts. It will help you move forward and beyond your problems.

Many of the resiliency factors make a difference in your life when you use them consistently over time. They make you more resilient as you apply them day in and day out. For instance, the tendency to be optimistic, getting enough sleep, and having self-control and self-discipline work this way.

But there are also resiliency factors that produce immediate results. I call them "Immediate-Impact Factors." They are factors that you can apply as you are going through stress that will have a positive effect on the amount of stress you are feeling. This happens through a cognitive, emotional, or a behavioral approach. Or, in layman's terms, these are approaches that exert conscious control of your thoughts, feelings, or actions.

For example, you can take a cognitive approach and change your perception of the problem by reframing it in a more positive light, or by getting out of the past or future and into the present moment. Or, if it's a minor stress, such as something that is just frustrating you, you can find the humor in it, and laugh at the situation.

An emotional approach could be to lean on your spirituality. Pray or connect with a higher power. Look at the problem with an eternal perspective or apply love and gratitude. What are you grateful for right now? Who are you grateful for? This can reduce stress immediately by changing your focus and feelings.

A behavioral approach could be doing a breathing exercise or going for some cardio exercise. This will produce a physiological change in your brain chemistry and adrenal glands, reducing the amount of stress hormones in your body.

The "Immediate-Impact Factors" are:

a. Live in the now – focus on the present moment (Cognitive)

b. Perception of problem – reframe it in a more positive light (Cognitive)

c. Sense of humor – is this something you can find humor in? (Cognitive)

d. Spirituality – connect with a higher power or look at the eternal perspective (Emotional)

e. Love and gratitude – focus on what and who you are grateful for right now (Emotional)

f. Body quieting – do a breathing exercise or meditation (Behavioral)

g. Fitness – go for a run or some other exercise (Behavioral)

h. Support system – talk to someone you trust

(Behavioral)

The *ADAPT to Succeed* Formula is an exercise that utilizes changes in your thoughts, feelings, or actions to reduce stress in the moment. If it's a minor stress, going through the formula once may be enough, but with more difficult trials you will have to run through the steps several times. It is an easy process once you get used to it, but you must practice it regularly in order to experience results. It will help with lowering stress and the negative outcomes of stress. It is a tool that will increase your capacity to handle high demands.

1. ACCEPT. You need to accept the situation that you are in. Don't give in to the "Why me?" syndrome or just wishing it wasn't happening. That is not helpful. You can't conquer the stress if you are stuck in denial.

    The Serenity Prayer reminds us;

    "God, Grant me the serenity to accept the things I cannot change,

    The courage to change the things I can,

    And the wisdom to know the difference."

    This step is about *accepting* the things you cannot change.

2. DECIDE. You need to decide that you are going to deal with this stress in a healthy way. Decide that you will be successful in dealing with it. There is power in just making that decision. There is power in thinking that this situation won't beat you, and that you will

emerge victorious in the end. This step is all about *committing* to a resilient response.

3. APPLY a FACTOR. This is where you get to choose an Immediate-Impact Factor, and apply it. Choose from:

   a. Live in the now – focus on the present moment

   b. Perception of problem – reframe it in a more positive light

   c. Sense of humor – is this something you can find humor in?

   d. Spirituality – connect with a higher power or look at the eternal perspective

   e. Love and gratitude – focus on what and who you are grateful for right now

   f. Body quieting – do a breathing exercise or meditation

   g. Fitness – go for a run or some other exercise

   h. Support system – talk to someone you trust

These are factors that can have an instant impact, so applying them now can reduce the stress you are feeling before you even get to step number four. Choose one that is effective for you. Not all these factors will have the same effect on everyone. We are all different. Some people want to talk it out, and some people want to go for a run. That's okay.

4.   PROBLEM-FOCUSED RESPONSE. This is where the other side of the Serenity Prayer comes into play. "The courage to change the things I can." Think about how you can exert some influence over the situation. This is where you are treating the root cause of the stress. What aspect of this situation can I control? You are applying the Active Coping Style here. You are not immobilized by this stress, you are not avoiding it, and you are deciding on a specific action you can take that will move you forward. This step is about taking positive action on the actual problem that is causing the stress. This is a problem-focused approach, as opposed to emotion-focused. Whatever you have to do, just lean into the pain and do it.

5.   TAKE STOCK. This is where you assess. Take stock of your feelings now. "How do I feel?" "Am I feeling less stress now?" "Is the problem getting better?" "Have I moved myself forward?" "Is it not as stressful now?" If it's a small problem, that may be all it takes for you to get to the point of saying, "I can handle this, it's no big deal." If it's a major stressor or an ongoing problem in your life, like going through a divorce, you will have to continue to go through these steps, maybe several times a day.

This method is not designed to eliminate all stressful feelings. It is designed to reduce the stress and the negative outcomes. And it is designed to help you take a positive approach, where you focus on the aspects that you can control and that will make you more resilient.

There are some situations that you will have more control over than other situations. Even if the situation is wholly out of your control, there will be some action that you can take. Although you may not control the situation itself, you can control how you think about it and how you respond to it. Taking some problem-solving action is more effective for resiliency than using only emotional coping on its own. This is because you are doing something to attack the root of the stress. So it's good to look for solutions and act on them. Using a repertoire of tools is better for increasing your immunity to stress than just using one tool. The most effective strategies for promoting resiliency involve multiple coordinated cognitive, emotional, and physiological approaches. The bolstering of more than one resiliency factor will have a greater effect on well-being.

EXAMPLES OF GOING THROUGH THE *ADAPT TO SUCCEED* FORMULA

You may want to use the *ADAPT to Succeed* Formula when you are facing mega-stress-related events such as divorce or a traumatic event. You can also use it when you face a minor frustration such as conflict in the workplace.

I will go through applying the formula now with a couple

of examples. But first I'll tell you about why I came up with this formula.

While I was going through the stress of my separation, I knew about the resiliency factors but I wasn't applying them. I knew certain things would help me, so why didn't I do those things? Intellectually knowing something isn't enough to gain the benefit. I wanted a tool or a formula that would make it simple to apply my knowledge. Like a guide to walk me through it. I experimented with different ways to apply the factors until I created this five-step formula. It worked. Then I created the ADAPT acronym so I could remember it. I consulted psychologists that are part of my network and went through the formula with them, using several different examples. They also thought it was a practical tool, and with a few minor recommended tweaks, it was an effective method to apply resilience to an immediate stressor. More importantly at the time, *it worked for me.*

Here are some examples of how to apply the formula.

EXAMPLE ONE:

I'm stressed with going through a separation and all that it entails.

Step 1. **Accept:** I have to accept it. I have to have enough wisdom to know when it's not something that can be reconciled. After a spouse leaves, some people will keep trying to get back together for months or years. It's good to try, but you have to know when to cut bait and move on. Accept that you are separated and will be getting divorced. It's over.

Step 2. **Decide:** I decide that I'm not going to be crushed by this. I'm not going to let this beat me. I commit to a resilient response!

Step 3. **Apply a factor:** I'm going to do some meditation. I need to quiet my body and mind. For 10 minutes, I meditate right now.

Step 4. **Problem-focused response:** Ok, what is it that is really stressing me? Well, one thing is the paperwork I have to prepare for my lawyer. I've been procrastinating. It's a painful process getting the financial statement together. I don't even like thinking about it, so I keep putting it off. But now I know I need to apply active coping. I figure out the next step. I plan the portion of the financial statement I can do at this point. I take action. I just bite the bullet and do the statement.

Step 5. **Take stock:** Now I assess how I feel. I feel better. I feel more confident that I have what it takes to get through this. I feel less stress. Tomorrow morning I may be back in the same boat, and will have to run through it again. I may go through it a few times a day, and then require it less and less as I build my resilience muscle. (And that is pretty much how it happened for me.)

EXAMPLE TWO:

I'm stressed because I have to fire somebody today.

Step 1. **Accept:** Yes, I accept it. I know I have to do it. No one's going to do it for me. I accept that.

Step 2. **Decide:** I decide that I'm a leader and a manager for a reason, and I'm committed to doing a good job of this. It's not for the faint of heart, but I know I can do this.

Step 3. **Apply a factor:** Support system. I'm going to call my cousin. I know in his business he has to fire people on a regular basis. I'll give him a call and just get some moral support. I'll see how he handles it. That will make me feel a little better, and help me see the big picture.

Step 4. **Problem-focused response:** I will plan out how I will do it. I will script what I'm going to say, so I don't get tongue-tied at the time. In fact, I'll plan to do a short role play with my admin assistant, to go through what I'm going to say and how I'll respond to objections or questions. That is actually a stress inoculation exercise and active coping, so it's doubling up on the resiliency factors. Now I lean in, and do it. By not attempting to avoid it, and by doing a good job of it, I experience less stress in the long run.

Step 5. **Take stock:** I'm feeling a high level of self-efficacy now. My stress is much lower than it was before.

It's the *ADAPT to Succeed* Formula because it will help you succeed if you follow it. It will help you achieve more by giving you a tool to overcome obstacles and withstand pressure. You'll be able to step up to the plate and be effective.

Now you try it. Take a stressor that you have in your life right now. Run through the formula.

Step 1. **Accept:** What is the stress? What do you need to accept?

Step 2. **Decide:** Commit to responding in a resilient way. Remember, there is power in decision.

Step 3. **Apply a factor:** Choose one of the immediate-impact factors. Which one will you do? Meditate? Change your perception of the problem? Take a few minutes right now and do it.

Step 4. **Problem-focused response:** What action can you take that will have an impact on the stress? What have you been putting off? What have you been avoiding that you know you have to do? What would make the problem smaller? If it can be done right now, put the book down and go do it!

Step 5. **Take stock:** How are you feeling? My guess is you feel more capable to deal with whatever is bothering you. If your stress was a nine out of ten before, and now it's a six out of ten, then that's success. This is not a miracle cure. It won't eliminate stress from your life. But it will make you better able to handle the stress. As you use this formula it will build your mental and emotional muscles so it will become easier to deal with the demands of life.

If it's the day after you found out your spouse cheated, or you just got fired or just experienced some other major trauma, don't get down on yourself if the formula doesn't work right away, or if you don't even feel like doing it. Sometimes in those moments you just want to freak out, maybe get drunk and cry. That's okay according to George Bonanno, Ph.D. It's what he calls "coping ugly" and although it's counterintuitive, sometimes it gets you through the toughest period. Sometimes the kindest thing you can do for yourself is to take a sleeping pill or Ativan and snow yourself under for a night. The key thing is not letting it turn into a long-term strategy. Don't let the pity party turn into a month-long bender. Allow yourself to experience "coping ugly" if you need to, but then pick yourself up and choose a healthier response.

When I went through my separation, the first couple of days were classic coping ugly. I'm glad George Bonanno gave me permission to be unhealthy for a few days. I wasn't capable of choosing a resilient response right at the start. But then I dusted myself off and decided to be resilient. There were still bad days, but by using the *ADAPT* Formula I got through it much better than I would have otherwise. The unhealthy coping gave way to healthy coping after a couple of days, instead of a couple months.

Life is difficult. It takes effort. Doing this formula will take effort. It takes effort to succeed. But make the effort. Then life will be less difficult. As we exert effort we are working towards creating a new reality that is better than the current reality.

This formula is not meant to take the place of professional counseling. Sometimes Step 4, the problem-focused response, is to get yourself in to see a psychologist or therapist. If you were raped or experienced the death of a child or other extreme trauma, go see a professional. The sooner you seek treatment, the more likely it is that you will recover fully. If you need counseling, set it up. That's part of having an active coping style.

Now that you've got a formula, use it to build your resiliency to enjoy a better quality of life. Use it to build your capacity to handle the slings and arrows of life.

CHAPTER TWENTY-SIX
PEAK PERFORMANCE

*"A ship in harbor is safe, but that is not
what ships are built for."*
John A. Shedd

Outstanding performance is not just a skillset. High performance is not based on ability as much as it depends on the mental state you are in. That is why some days you perform well and some days you perform poorly. You have the same ability, but your mental state can vary. When you are in a confident and powerful state you will perform better than when you're feeling stressed and overwhelmed. So the key is to be able to control your inner dialog, your focus and confidence, even when the pressure is on.

Hendrie Weisinger, Ph.d., and J.P. Pawliw-Fry did a multi-year study where they researched individuals who were top performers across vastly different fields from business to sports.[59] They looked at over 10,000 people, and then sought

59) Weisinger, H., Pawliw-Fry, J.P. (2015). Performing Under Pressure: The Science of Doing Your Best When it Matters Most. New York: Crown Business.

out what made the top 10 percent different from the other 90 percent. What separated the CEO from middle-managers? What separated LeBron James and Tom Brady from other very talented people in their sports? The result of the study was that they determined one consistent trait had a greater impact on peak performance than any other trait, and all the best-of-the-best had this trait: *The ability to perform under pressure.* Their research demonstrated that stress and pressure have a negative impact on everyone, but the most successful people were able to manage that pressure better than the rest. Two people with similar talent and ability may perform in a similar way from day to day, but when the pressure is on, when the stakes are high, the one will thrive and the other will choke. That's what sets apart the great ones in business or sports. Learning to perform better under stress and pressure will give you an advantage in whatever field you are in.

WHAT IS PEAK PERFORMANCE?

The Dictionary of Sport and Exercise Science and Medicine states that, "Peak performance is a state in which the person performs to the maximum of their ability, characterized by subjective feelings of confidence, effortlessness and total concentration on the task."[60] The resiliency factors that we discussed equip you to perform confidently while keeping the stress in check.

---

60) Peak performance. (n.d.) Dictionary of Sport and Exercise Science and Medicine by Churchill Livingstone. (2008). Retrieved January 30 2015 from http://medical-dictionary.thefreedictionary.com/peak+performance.

YERKES-DODSON THEORY

Yerkes-Dodson Theory demonstrates the relationship between stress and performance. Kendra Cherry in the article *What is the Yerkes-Dodson Law and How Does It Work?* says,

> "The Yerkes-Dodson Law suggests that there is a relationship between performance and arousal (stress). Increased arousal can help improve performance, but only up to a certain point. At the point when arousal becomes excessive, performance diminishes.
>
> The law was first described in 1908 by psychologists Robert Yerkes and John Dillingham Dodson. They discovered that mild electrical shocks could be used to motivate rats to complete a maze, but when the electrical shocks became too strong, the rats would scurry around in random directions to escape. The experiment demonstrated that increasing stress and arousal levels could help focus motivation and attention on the task at hand, but only up to a certain point."[61]

For example, if you are facing a deadline at work, the closer it gets to that deadline the more stress you experience, which actually improves your performance. You would get more accomplished. But then if your boss started screaming at you also, that would be too much stress and your performance would decline. The bottom line is that some stress is good, but

61) Cherry, K. (n.d.). What Is the Yerkes-Dodson Law and How Does It Work? Retrieved January 30, 2015, from http://psychology.about.com/od/yindex/f/yerkes-dodson-law.htm.

too much stress is bad.

There is a zone in the middle where we have the right amount of stress to perform at our best. That is the sweet spot where we achieve our peak performance. If you move beyond that sweet spot, and have exceedingly high demands, that's when you get overwhelmed or burned out.

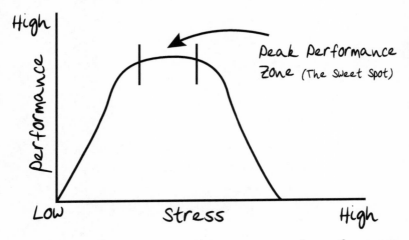

As we increase our resilience, our peak performance zone widens. The top of the inverse U plateaus or flattens out, and extends farther and gives us greater latitude in the sweet spot. This gives you a heightened ability to succeed when the demands are high. That is why resiliency leads to success. That is why resiliency is more critical to your success than education or training or experience. When you have a higher level of resilience, you have a higher capacity to work in a psychologically demanding environment while still being in your peak performance zone.

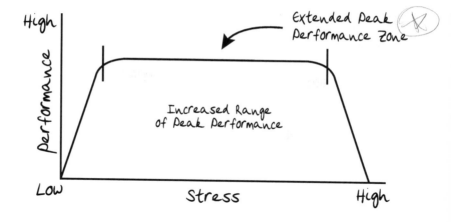

Increased resilience equals an increased peak performance zone

Remember, in order to achieve your biggest goals, <u>maximizing your performance while under stress is key</u>.

RECOVERY TIME

Although you can increase your ability to work at your peak under stress, it cannot continue steadily and unceasingly. I like to compare it to a weightlifter. You can't handle an ever-increasing stress load any more than a weightlifter can handle an ever-increasing weight without rest. Body builders can increase their muscle and adapt to heavier weights, but it's a gradual process that requires recovery time. Once you've maxed out what you can lift, you add a little more weight at a time and then rest and recover, and eventually you will have increased your capacity. It's the same with mental and emotional muscles. After a stressful period, take time to relax, because burnout is the result of chronic unceasing pressure. Practice working under slightly increased pressure and it will get easier and your capacity will grow.

> *"Uncertainty   and   fear   are   relieved*
> *by   authority.   Training   is   authority."*
> *– Ryan Holiday, The Obstacle is the Way*

INCREASED CAPACITY UNDER PRESSURE

A good example of this is the Sderot story discussed earlier in the book. Previously, I spoke about the effect of The Red Color Song in lowering stress and increasing resilient outcomes, such as reduced PTSD. But now I'm going to speak about it in relation to *performance under pressure*. The Red Color Song[62] is sung by children as they respond to Kassam rocket attacks. Their performance is critical because when the Red Color alarm sounds, indicating a pending rocket attack, these young children have 15 seconds to run to shelter. If they don't make it to shelter in 15 seconds, the outcome can be significant injury or death. The translation of the song is:

Red Color Song,
by Shahar Bar, an Art Therapist near Sderot, Israel

Red color, red color.

Hurry, hurry, hurry to a safe area.

Hurry, hurry, hurry 'cause now it's a bit dangerous.

---

62) Go to https://www.youtube.com/watch?v=1YueeDYVdgk to see the actual song performed.

My heart is beating boom, boom, boom.

My body is shaking boom, boom, boom.

But I am overcoming 'cause I am a little different.

Falling down—we may now stand up.

Our body we shake, shake, shake.

Our legs we loosen, loosen, loosen.

Breathe in deep, breathe out far.

Breathe in deep. We can laugh ha, ha, ha.

It's all gone and I feel good it's over.

Yesssss!

Before they had this song to help them perform, many children would start crying. They wouldn't know what to do, and many would freeze and just stand there, wherever they were in the playground. The alarm would be wailing and many would choke.

However, using this song helped them:

- To know what to do (hurry to a safe area)

- Downplay the stress and pressure of it (it's a *bit* dangerous)

- To recognize and normalize the stress reaction (shaking body)

- Increase confidence (I am overcoming)

- Reduce the feelings of stress once the danger is gone (deep breathing and laughing)

More children get to safety now. The children don't freeze or choke under pressure anymore. The stakes are high and they perform well despite the stress. This is an example of how increasing your resilience can help your performance when it matters most.

GRIT

I couldn't end this chapter on peak performance without discussing grit. There is new research that suggests that your level of success is determined more by grit than intelligence, ability, or talent. There are a number of definitions of grit and what components make up grit, but most agree that resilience is part of it. Experts say that it's a composite of traits such as determination, passion, courage, perseverance, resilience, and a willingness to take risks. Grittiness is essential for success.

It reminds me of a part in the movie *Full Metal Jacket* when Private Joker was being yelled at by Gunnery Sgt. Hartman. Private Joker wouldn't back down, so Gunnery Sgt. Hartman fired the squad leader and promoted Private Joker to squad leader. In doing so, he yelled one of his all-time great lines, "Private Joker is silly and he's ignorant, but he's got guts, and guts is enough!" I always loved that line. When my daughter was a stubborn and headstrong four-year-old and would do something nonsensical, I would yell at her, "Melissa, you're silly and you're ignorant, but you've got guts, and guts is enough!" I think that made me a good father. I could be wrong.

But the world is big, mean, and tough. As I watched her leave home to go to University, knowing she'd be living alone in a big city, I had confidence knowing that her gritty, gutsy attitude would be more important than her GPA in determining whether she was successful or not.

Outstanding performance is built on heart and mindset. In the 1996 Olympics Kerri Strug was part of the USA Gymnastics Team and competing in the vault. She injured her ankle badly during one vault. In order for the US team to win the gold medal, Kerri would have to vault again, despite her injury. This 18-year-old girl ran, vaulted, and landed on both feet despite what they found out was a third-degree lateral sprain and tendon damage. Her coach carried her to the podium where she and her team got the gold medal. She should have been out with an injury like that. When it came to that last vault that clinched the gold medal, it was courage and grit and heart that made the difference.

HOOAH!

I like to watch movies about Navy Seals, Delta Force, or other elite units. Movies like *Act of Valor*, *American Sniper*, *Blackhawk Down*, and *Lone Survivor*. It amazes me how well elite warriors perform under incredibly demanding situations. Their peak performance zone on the Yerkes-Dodson chart would be well beyond most people's capacity to perform. Through training, they have extended the upper limits of stress that they can work with and still perform.

The more you train yourself in building the various resiliency factors, the more mental and emotional toughness you will have. You will be able to perform better under pressure and be more impervious to uncertainty, fear, and stress. That will increase your success in all aspects of life.

CHAPTER TWENTY-SEVEN
PTG
(POST-TRAUMATIC GROWTH)

"To grow our muscles, we must strain our body,
To grow in knowledge, we must strain our mind,
To grow in character, we must strain our soul."
Brad Coulbeck

Post-Traumatic Growth (PTG) refers to positive changes that occur as a result of coping with a traumatic event. It happens when you bounce back from trauma, but bounce to a higher level than you were at before. Dr. Martin Seligman states that "The *usual* response to trauma and adversity is growth." Isn't it great that our minds are designed to adapt and grow from stress? It's just like our muscles growing when they are burdened.

Health psychologist Kelly McGonigal reveals that having a negative attitude about stress may be bad for your health: "Can changing how you think about stress make you healthier?

Here the science says yes," says McGonigal. "Your heart might be pounding, you may be breathing faster... but what if you viewed them as signs that your body was energized and it's preparing you to meet this challenge?" She says making this paradigm shift in your thinking could be lifesaving.

STRESS MAY ACTUALLY BE CORRELATED WITH LONGEVITY—IF A PERSON DOESN'T VIEW IT AS A NEGATIVE.

Researchers at the University of Wisconsin-Madison asked approximately 29,000 people to rate their level of stress over the past year and how much they believed this stress influenced their health. Over the next eight years the researchers studied public death records to record the passing of any subjects. They found that people who reported having high levels of stress, and who believed stress had a large impact on their health, had a whopping 43% increased risk of death. On the other hand, those who experienced a lot of stress but did not perceive its effects as negative were amongst the least likely to die as compared to all other participants in the study.[63]

If you believe all stress is bad and will do bad things to you, chances are it will make you sick. If you believe that stress is normal and that you can deal with it, chances are you won't get sick. Likewise, with PTSD there is a placebo effect. If people believe that PTSD is the normal reaction to trauma, they increase their chance of experiencing PTSD after a traumatic

---

63) Stress as a positive: Recent research that suggests it has benefits. (2013, September 4). Retrieved January 30, 2015, from http://blog.ted.com/2013/09/04/could-stress-be-good-for-you-recent-research-that-suggests-it-has-benefits/.

incident. Beliefs create a self-fulfilling prophecy. The placebo effect is well documented and has a significant impact on either improving or diminishing your health, depending on your mindset.

W. Keith Campbell, a professor of social psychology at the University of Georgia said, "Really negative events have the ability to shake up the status quo in your life, which opens the door for change. You could become a depressed, despairing drunk—or you could become a much better person."

People are transformed by trauma but their perception dictates whether that transformation is positive or negative. PTG can help you reach a new level of being, but it comes with a price. The price is the trauma you suffered and the work that you do to actively recover and find meaning in your experience. Increase your potential for PTG by understanding it and looking for growth. Believe and have faith that you will grow and it will help you move forward. If you look for growth, you will find growth. You find what you focus on!

Richard Tedeschi of the University of North Carolina said there are elements that can lead to PTG. If you do these things, it can increase the likelihood that you will experience growth:

- Understand the response to trauma.

- Reduce anxiety through body quieting and relaxation.

- Speak to a therapist or otherwise talk it out with someone in your support system.

- Find meaning in the suffering, and look for gains.

- Look at it in the perspective of life's journey, and

understand the hero's journey. (To be discussed in the following chapter.)

Based on informal surveys that I have conducted, I've found that almost everyone has heard of PTSD (Post-Traumatic Stress Disorder), but almost no one has heard of PTG (Post-Traumatic Growth). This is surprising, considering that PTG is much more prevalent than PTSD. Most people who go through a major trauma do not get PTSD or other psychological disorders. They recover fully. People are naturally resilient for the most part. When we hear stats like "15% of the soldiers returning from combat develop PTSD," it means that 85% did not. So I look at that in a positive way...the glass is 85% full.

There have been studies indicating that 30 to 50 percent of people *actually grow* from whatever trauma they experienced. They are better human beings in some way due to the adversity that they were able to pass through.

I sometimes see social media posts or articles about how the authors want to raise awareness of PTSD. I don't agree, and here's why. Virtually everyone is already aware of PTSD. And awareness of PTSD is just the awareness of what can go wrong, the awareness of the negative outcome. What's missing is an awareness of PTG and resiliency. Far fewer people are aware of the positive outcomes. And awareness of resiliency factors and positive outcomes will be what has the most impact on preventing PTSD in the first place.

GROWTH

When people experience growth, it doesn't mean they didn't suffer or go through a period of distress. They may have suffered intensely, with their entire worldview shattered. But it does mean that they had positive changes resulting from the event and its aftermath.

Tedeschi and Calhoun have found in their research that people commonly report growing in these five areas:

- A greater appreciation for life
- More meaningful interpersonal relationships
- Enhanced spiritual beliefs
- New direction and purpose in life
- An increased sense of personal strength

Odds are in your favor that you will experience growth as opposed to PTSD if you are touched by tragedy. To tilt the scales in your favor even more, just make a conscious decision that you will gain something positive. There is power in simply deciding that you will overcome. Decide that you will find meaning in your suffering, and that you will grow in one of the ways I mentioned above.

I like what Phil Stutz and Barry Michels said about Nietzsche's quote, "That which does not kill you makes you stronger." In their book *The Tools*, the authors wrote, "Nietzsche's statement makes it sound like adversity itself makes you stronger. It doesn't. Inner strength comes only to those who *move forward* in the face of adversity."[64]

64) Stutz P., Michels B. (2012) The Tools: 5 Tools to help you find courage, creativity, and willpower – and inspire you

If someone doesn't move forward, if they get stuck and can't move past the "why me" stage, if they are wallowing in the pain, and that is their only story, we call that person a victim. The victim mentality is a state where someone refuses to put forth any effort to grow and move forward.

Resilient individuals experience adversity, then they rise to the challenge, they learn, they grow, and they succeed. I'm not saying trauma is good or that we should welcome it into our lives, but when it does find us, don't wallow in self-pity. Become a better person.

to live life in forward motion. New York. Spiegel & Grau.

Chapter Twenty-Eight
The Success Journey

"Far better is it to dare mighty things, to win glorious
triumphs, even though checkered by failure...
than to rank with those poor spirits who neither enjoy
nor suffer much, because they live in a gray twilight
that knows not victory nor defeat."
Theodore Roosevelt

Pain, pleasure and progress are all a part of life. You can't go through your journey here on Earth not expecting things to go sideways every so often. What makes a person successful is not that they had an easy life, but that they faced struggle and adversity and were able to overcome it.

Warren Bennis, leadership author and founding chairman of The Leadership Institute at the University of Southern California, had this to say: "The leaders I met, whatever walk of life they were from, whatever institutions they were presiding over, always referred back to the same failure—something that happened to them that was personally difficult, even traumatic, something that made them feel that desperate sense of hitting bottom—as something they thought was almost a necessity. It's as if at that moment the iron entered their soul; that moment created the resilience that leaders need."

It's not about surviving challenge and adversity. It's about thriving. You can get kicked in the teeth and not only survive, but grow and flourish. Everyone faces trauma in life, to different extents. It's what you do with it that matters.

We can learn how resilience is a critical ingredient in success from studying great people. I've always liked reading biographies of leaders and brilliant people. Before I knew about the resiliency factors, I didn't put the equation together, about how those who eventually became leaders in their field usually had to struggle against great odds and become better as they were forced to deal with adversity. These people often say that they had to go through tribulations to become who they were in the end, and would not have made it without the growth and insight earned through trials. I realized a lot of them were great because of their level of resiliency, which gave them the mental and emotional toughness to overcome whatever obstacles were in front of them. All of them in their own way had to possess the ability to bounce back from adversity.

One example was Winston Churchill, who experienced political and military embarrassment due to implementing poor war strategies, leaving him responsible for huge military disasters in World War 1. He was able to get through disaster and embarrassment by facing a personal reality that would have stopped most people: overcoming massive public failure. He struggled and eventually did it. He became the greatest Prime Minister England has ever had, and was a brilliant war strategist in World War 2. That is what he is remembered for.

Abraham Lincoln continually lost political elections and eventually won the presidency because of his tenacity. There are so many more that I could cite as resiliency role models. Look at Oprah, born into poverty in rural Mississippi to a teenage single mother, raped at age 9, pregnant at 14, and losing her son in infancy. She would have had all the excuses to not become the most successful woman in entertainment. Resiliency is a huge part of her success.

Look at Steve Jobs. What made him great? There is no doubt that Steve Jobs was an outstanding business leader. But what was it about him that made him great? Was it his genius at tech development, his creativity, his vision, his knack for marketing? Sure, it was likely a combination of all those things. What always impressed me with Steve Jobs, though, was his resilience, his persistence, his ability to bounce back, his grit, and his unflagging enthusiasm.

Here's a man who was fired from the company that he founded. He was fired by the CEO that he himself had hired. I'd hate to have to come home and explain that to my wife! He had other failures over the years: the Lisa computer, the Apple 3, the NeXT computer (which was a commercial failure), and the Newton platform. Then there were his serious health problems, being diagnosed with cancer in 2004. Clearly, his success was no cakewalk.

He fought through all his failures, challenges, and obstacles to become the Henry Ford of our day. It's not just the MacBooks, iPods, iPads, and iPhones either. Steve changed the entire music industry with iTunes and the movie industry with Pixar. If Steve Jobs had not been resilient, he would have been crushed by his early defeats instead of going on to become the icon that he is. He is an example to everyone who has ever been fired, who has invested in ideas that tanked, or has suffered with health problems while continuing to work.

There are others I respect such as Teddy Roosevelt, Victor Frankl, Henry Morton Stanley, and Malala Yousafzai, just to name a few. These are people that I've looked up to. None of them would be known if it wasn't for their capacity to thrive despite trauma and obstacles. I've been able to look at their lives to determine what factors made them successful, then I tried to model that in my life. Modeling successful people is inspiring and one of the best ways to achieve success yourself.

THE HERO'S JOURNEY

The Hero's Journey is as old as the human experience. It *is* the human experience. In Joseph Campbell's seminal work, *The Hero with a Thousand Faces* first published in 1949, he compares myths and stories from ancient cultures around the world. There are commonalities in story structures from different ages and vastly different cultures. One common aspect of myths and stories going back thousands of years is that the protagonist always faces tests or obstacles that have to be overcome. If people across all cultures and all times have faced adversity, why is it that we feel we should be spared? Why should the current generation be exempted from struggle? I find it helpful to remember when I am going through a difficult time that it is the normal human experience, and how I face my trials will be the determination of my character.

> *"Nurture your mind with great thoughts. To believe in the heroic makes heroes."*
> *– Benjamin Disraeli*

People love to watch a story with struggle, with adversity. Think of your favorite movie, and remove the adversity. There is no more movie without it. My favorite movie is Braveheart, but without the war, without the struggle against tyranny, it would not be heroic. Imagine if Darth Vader was a good father, or imagine if Jaws was a dolphin, or if the Terminator came back to hang out with John Connor. Boring!

Life is struggle, but we know instinctively that that is the juice of life. A life without struggle is an unlived life. There must be dragons to slay in your life.

> *"If you banish the dragons, you banish the heroes."*
> *– Andrew Solomon, TED 2014*

TRANSCENDING THE STORM

A few years ago, when I was the ERT Team Leader in northern Ontario, I had to fly from Hearst to Moosonee, a remote village on James Bay that has no roads running to it, to pick up a prisoner. I was alone in a nine-passenger plane except for the pilot and copilot. It was in the winter, at night, and in the middle of a blinding snowstorm. All I could see was swirling snow.

I was worried. When we were taking off we had no visibility, we couldn't see anything except night and the snow. I thought we could crash. As we were gaining altitude I was looking out the window into darkness and blowing snow. It seemed lonely in the passenger compartment of this plane. I had some dark feelings, fear, uncertainty, and felt alone in this remote, stormy sky. But as we continued to climb to our 18,000-foot cruising altitude, we went above the storm. I could look down and see the storm clouds below me. Where I was now was clear and bright. The stars were sparkling and the northern lights were swirling across the sky.

It was beautiful. It had an immediate impact on my emotions. I was overcome with gratitude for this experience. Being alone in the dark and surrounded by the northern lights, I now felt peace, comfort, and tranquility. I enjoyed the beauty of it. I felt close to the Creator. It was a profound experience. I realized that everyone else was in a snowstorm down below. No one but the pilots and I could see this. It was there all along. It's just that no one knew because no one else could see it from our current perspective. They weren't at 18,000 feet.

I don't remember how long the flight was, but the whole time I watched the northern lights and felt a deep sense of gratitude. I thought about how my perspective changed so quickly by getting above the clouds. Changing my perspective changed how I saw the world and changed how I felt. It became a metaphor for me. All I could see was darkness and the storm, until I could get above it. When I elevated my view, when I transcended the storm, there was beauty and peace.

When we are caught up in our day-to-day stress, all we can see is the storm. By focusing on gratitude and elevating our thoughts we can break through the clouds and see what is really there. We can see the deeper truth of the situation. It enables us to see the beauty that always exists in the world, but which we sometimes choose not to see, because it's easier to see the storm.

We can rise above our current dark space by nurturing ourselves with positive thoughts and feelings. This world can be stormy and dark, as it always has been throughout history, but there are ways to protect our hearts and minds and emerge victorious. We all have strength deep within us that is superior to whatever circumstance we are facing. Cultivate resiliency, experience the joy in *your* hero's journey, and you will achieve success. That is the power of a resilient mind.

ACKNOWLEDGEMENTS

First I'd like to thank Dr. Bill McDermott and Dr. Lori Gray for piquing my interest in resiliency many years ago, and then answering hundreds of questions since then. I want to thank Dr. Danny Brom, the Director of the Israel Center for the Treatment of Psychotrauma, and Dr. Ruth Pat-Horenczyk, the Director or Research at the ICTP, not only for information, but also inspiration.

I want to acknowledge Sharon Jenkins for writing and editing guidance, and for giving me a kick in the butt when I procrastinated. Thanks to my mother and two sisters, Jackie, Leah and Stacy, for reading draft copies and providing editing suggestions. They are teachers and love to mark grammar errors in red. Thanks to Maureen Geddes for her very insightful suggestions.

I also want to thanks Rose Adams and Greg Schinkel for inspiring me and pushing me. Finally I want to thank Jen, Corynn and Natalie for moral support and encouragement as I wrote this book over the last three years while working full time. Without their belief in this project, it never would have materialized.

74036834R00144

Made in the USA
San Bernardino, CA
12 April 2018